HAVE FAITH

or

*how to build
your Micro-Utopia
and save the planet*

Mag Ela

First published in 2019

© 2019 Mag Ela/The House of Eleima All rights reserved

Otropos Press
P.O. Box 15 914
1001 NK Amsterdam, The Netherlands

www.eleima.org

ISBN 978-0-244-17536-8

HAVE FAITH

or

*how to build
your Micro-Utopia
and save the planet*

Mag Ela

Otropos Press
2019

Love is all around.
You can feel it in the air.

Contents

Introduction 1

A brief history of the world: Where we come from 17

A brief history of the world revisited: How The Consciousness came into being 20

Man walks among us 27

Do you believe in magic? 34

The awful truth 38

You gotta have Faith 46

Epicurus the prophet, or We don't need this fascist groove thang 53

We need to talk about Gods 61

The language of The Faith 65

A bit of a myth 68

People 72

What are we talking about here? 74

The Eternal Heart 80

The Faith shows a way out of the madness 82

Next stop: reincarnation! 88

- Love and Beauty 93
- Mag Ela 99
- The Snake of Chaos rears its ugly head again 103
- The war of the Gods 108
- The falling leaves 124
- A Contract of Social Joy 131
- Privacy, property, responsibility 136
- The good merchant 141
- Before travelling to Utopia 153
- Establishing a temple of joy 161
- Non-violence 165
- Slow down 171
- Do not hold a grudge 175
- True luxury 181
- So you'd like to change the world? 185
- A beginning, an end 190
- The body is the gate 194
- One last thing 201
- Further reading 205
- Soundtrack 206

*"Here is your crown
And your seal and rings.
And here is your love
For all things."*

- Leonard Cohen, 'Here it is'

Introduction

In the spring of 2016 I fell asleep at the wheel, and I drove my car into the crash barrier at 80 mph. Waking from the loud noise, I sped on, barely blinking. One week later, I got involved with a British artist, who managed to shatter my self-confidence, expose my thinking as fraudulent, and subsequently left me believing my goals were no more than empty pursuits. Something sweet gone sour was nothing I hadn't tasted before, but now I couldn't even go for a drive.

Thinking back on the moment before I crashed, in a split second between being lost in sleep and coming to my senses, I sensed something holding me. I was aware that I could have been snuffed out like a candle without even noticing it, but instead, there had been something going on, and it wasn't to do with that sweet sleep of death. It had felt like dissolving in a bath of ink, watching the undertow of the void. In that moment I had clearly and distinctly felt the notion of something living in what is supposed to be the realm of absolute nothingness. It felt like having gone under in something that was watching me with a certain sense of curiosity. What had happened, what had I seen? I had the vague notion of having seen Love itself foreshadowing its appearance, and not in a kind way.

As I tried to regain my composure, I found myself thinking about the things that make up life. Not just your everyday work-buy-consume-die-life, but The Good Life. How to find peace of mind? Some say it's money that brings peace of mind, some say it's a well-ordered house. Others say it's being able to live in a country where the enemy can be easily identified, and then there are those who claim 'Zen' is the answer. None of these routes seemed very attractive to me. I couldn't sit still for over a minute, I didn't care about classifying others as enemies, and I had enough money not to have to worry too much. For all I knew, I was living the good life such as it was, and I just didn't notice it, being wrapped up in thoughts of love and death.

Luckily, we live in an age in which roadmaps to happiness are for sale, so I went out to look at what was on offer. It wasn't much of a success. There were so many roads that I got dizzy just thinking about actually having to travel into that world of the good. It seemed to me that this overly mapped world was just another form of anarchy, and anarchy has never been conducive to peace of mind. An anarchic state is basically the precursor to panic, and with panic coming on, it was easy for me to see that the good life was slipping away. So, in my search for peace of mind, I realised I wasn't looking for a roadmap to happiness, I was merely looking to find something that would show me who I was and what I needed to do.

Looking around me, I was surprised to find the others didn't feel lost too. My friends seemed to have fun, my colleagues went on working same as always. I looked out of my office window, I watched tourists walk past, laughing and trudging their suitcases. Everything seemed fine. The shops displayed clothes at bargain prices, and if happiness wasn't for sale, at least you could look good while feeling unhappy - but then, why would you feel unhappy if there was all this beauty at bargain prices? And if clothes didn't do it for you, you could always binge-watch tales of murder and mayhem, dive into the world of '50 shades', or watch Batman try to murder Superman. What's not to like? What's not to keep you with a permanent smile on your face? - but I wasn't smiling and it now all seemed madness to me.

Was I going through a crisis? I don't think so. All I wanted was to get a grip on myself, just to re-establish a clear border between being dead and being alive. I had seen a darkness. I had loved. I had lost. I had felt the presence of a world living, yet invisible. What annoyed me was that I hadn't had any kind of system in place to make sense of these unconnected events that had somehow become connected. Come to think of it, I didn't even have any guidelines to help me think of ways to behave in a crisis, not just in a crisis of love, but not in any crisis. I was a babe in the woods, a ship cast adrift, or simply put: I was a modern, nihilistic citizen of the consumer state, with nothing to hold on to, other than a vague notion of emotional stability, a notion that was eluding me even as I seemingly continued with my daily routine. This was not a satisfying state to be in.

"I always wondered how long it 'd be before you turned to smack or God," sang my favourite Australian Ed Kuepper, and it seemed to me there was the answer. I didn't feel like heroin, so it was to be God. I started reading the holy books, and the books do have much to offer, but I couldn't get myself past their history. The fabric of many a book has been stained through the bloody acts of its adherents. Besides, I soon discovered I wasn't merely looking for a religious education, instead, I was searching for a guide. I wasn't searching for words in a book that had already been interpreted to death. And as for the hip priests, I wasn't looking for someone telling me what they themselves had picked up along the way. I wanted something new, a teaching that was bold, fresh and profound. I wasn't a lost soul looking to be saved, I just want something to hold on to other than smack.

A line of Karl Marx rang in my ears: "All that is solid turns into air." It's from the infamous Communist Manifesto, and it refers to the way capitalism by its nature can't ever stand still, and ultimately must destroy what it creates. I never actually read 'The Communist Manifesto', but I'm pretty sure Marx' vision was spot-on. These days it's becoming abundantly clear that capitalism is a monster leading all of us on a road to ruin. Marx was right, but again, his teachings have been stained. Yet something that had once seemed solid to me had now dissolved, and I was lost. So Marx seemed a possible guide, albeit a slightly shady one.

Then I started noticing things aren't what they seemed. The world keeps on turning sure enough, but no one is at ease. For starters, there is climate change, or 'global warming' as we used to call it. A few years ago, the news merely mentioned vague things like 'maybe sea level rise at the end of the 21st century', and you'd think, 'Well, fine, after me, the floods' - but you can't do that anymore. It has now become obvious that one metre of sea-level rise is a best case scenario. Already we're dealing with a best case in which vast swaths of land have become uninhabitable, and the worst is still to come. Climate change is happening all around us, but then there is global capitalism, too. The industry responsible seems to be hell-bent on producing more planes, trains and automobiles - maybe they're thinking we can all out-perform the four horsemen of the Apocalypse.

Plus, it seems obvious there's something wrong when 60 or so people own half the world's riches. Even when it doesn't seem to matter much if the earth we walk on is owned by some billionaire instead of by an oil company, this ownership brings with it the notion of armies and starvation.

And if you'd like to believe that our leaders might come to their senses, sad to say, there really don't seem to be any leaders anymore, it's all just market forces and politicians paying lip service to change or blaming all our current woes on poor refugees running for their lives. On top of that, there is, or was, the animal world. Species are disappearing all over the planet, either hunted to extinction, poisoned, or simply chased off and left to die by the ever more aggressive agricultural industry.

So, things aren't fine. And as I was nursing my broken heart, I could see that, in fact, they were awful. I found myself pondering the undercurrent of death, because thinking about life was just too depressing.

Then suddenly, it all erupted, but not quite in the way you would expect. I noticed that Jim

Carrey had happened. A famous comedian who started preaching along the lines of ancient Hindu wisdom, no less. Jim Carrey was 'Woke', or so I understood. He had woken up. "There is no Self," Carrey said, "It's a mask we put on. There is just a relative manifestation of consciousness that someone has given a name. This name becomes 'your personality', but it's not real. Once you see that you are already a complete manifestation, everything else is just a game" - something like that anyway. From acting, he went to painting, and it seemed life was good for the people who were woke - you'd think we would all want to be woke, especially if we could all be millionaire actors as well.

However, the internet had people crying 'Has Jim Carrey gone mad?!' Millions of people sought out esoteric leanings as well as criticisms of those leanings. It was fascinating. I didn't know what to think of any of it, but 50,000,000 Jim Carrey fans can't be wrong, I figured, nor can an equal number of critics. However, then something happened that made Jim Carrey not seem so very relevant anymore. Donald Trump got elected as president of the United States of America. In many ways, Trump is the anti-Carrey. He has lots of Self, which we'll conveniently call 'Ego', and he's an obnoxious billionaire making poor immigrants take the blame for the poverty of desperate Americans. Donald Trump wasn't

Woke, but unlike Jim Carrey, he had become emperor of the Western world. At once, ersatz-Donalds started to pop up - a deeply troubling notion.

Finally, back in my own life, I became aware how quite a few of my friends had had nervous breakdowns. It turned out half were on anti-depressants, and some had been on anti-depressants for years and they weren't about to stop. Not just my friends, also acquaintances, friends of friends, and acquaintances of friends, and acquaintances of acquaintances - everyone, really. The artist that had caused my heartbreak had also been on anti-depressants. The anti-depressant industry is booming, and I never paid it any mind - but when I started doing so, it made perfect sense to me. We all feel something is coming at us, we all feel reality is becoming ever more surreal, we all feel everything that once was solid has dissolved into air. We're not depressed, we worry, and we have good reason to. The main problem seems to be, you can't tell the depressed this, because they don't feel so great as it is, and it's pointless to tell the others, because they pretend they don't know what you're talking about. And If they do know, they either don't want to know or they don't care.

So there I was. I wasn't woke. I wasn't on anti-depressants, but I could easily see why all of us really should be depressed, and desperately needed to wake up. And my car was still nowhere near getting repaired.

And that's where it's at. "Everything's a little upside down, as a matter of fact, the wheels have stopped," to quote Bob Dylan. I might add that things aren't just upside down, nothing seems to be in the right place anymore. It's been three years since my crash, and crazy is the new normal. Maybe it's just that the wool that had been pulled over our collective eyes has gone up in flames. Maybe Jim Carrey is still the only one who's woke, and all the others are sleep-walking towards a cliff, including yours truly. Either way, it's become abundantly clear to everyone but the most stoic that collectively, mankind has entered into an age of chaos that's akin to well, maybe the 1930's - and we know how that ended. People longed for security, and instead they got fascism.

Now, the attraction of fascism isn't hard to see. It's been pointed out that the fascists have all the best lines. They wear nice clothes, they're not afraid to call an enemy an enemy, they don't mind a bit of violence, and what's more, they offer an alternative to feeling helpless. Fascism is empowering. Fascism tells you life can be good if not for the enemy causing your woes.

The modern-day fascist incantation goes something like this: 'We've worked hard in the past; now there is no longer any work because of the poor people doing the work for next to nothing; so we need to get rid of the poor people and then we can all work hard again.' As if the promise of hard labour is such an attractive thing, but it's a lie to boot. Still, it has a history. Fascism is steeped in blood and anger, and there has always been plenty of that.

It's not a great idea to join the fascists, but I can see the attraction. Fascism may be a little more insidious than I make it out to be, but not a lot. Instead of struggling to change the awful reality into a better one, it probably makes sense to just push your boat into that river of blood and peddle along with the crowd. An attractive fantasy is clearly more attractive than a depressing reality. To avoid the pitfalls of fascism, it's of the utmost importance that daily life becomes a source of pleasure again. To that end, what we need is to find is our way back to 'the good life'. Without a notion of what the good life consists of though, it's easy to see that something else will be our reality soon, and that might not be such a wonderful thing.

By now you might ask, 'What's the connection between your car, the coming Apocalypse, lost love, searching for God, comedians being Woke, and fascists on the move?'

Well, I'll tell you.

In search of The Good Life, I was thinking about Gods in a jokey sort-of way. It's just that

I wasn't laughing so very hard, and no one laughed along.

This got me thinking about 'Love' not as a feeling, but as a force. People regularly talk about Love as if it's an independent thing. Just think of songs with titles like 'Love is going to lift you up', or 'Love is all around'. And I thought, well, what if 'Love' really is a force that is out in the world, looking for people to express itself? What if this feeling is in fact the way I experienced being used by this force? Love had not lifted me up, it had got me down. Maybe that was because Love just wanted to make itself known. It didn't care for me, it just cared for my feelings showing, whether happy or sad. Maybe Love just wants to propagate the same way as chickens or roses do.

What did that make me, what does that make us? It means we're a vessel, a mode of transport for Love - who knows, maybe we should think of ourselves as the flowers of this invisible but very present force. And just like flowers, we have a function, namely to further the Love. Love may break your heart occasionally, that's true, but that's just a figure of speech. A heart doesn't really break, it merely gets dented somewhat, and Love goes on because of us acting in a loving way.

However, if there is an independent force called 'Love' that is using us, it makes sense its opposite is also out there in the world. Now, what is the opposite of 'Love'? I would say it's

'Evil'. When I look around, I see there is indeed quite a bit of evil being expressed. The people who are willing to make a fast buck out of killing the last rhinoceros, the politicians willing to let the oil industry poison entire countries, the policemen who will blow up their fellow citizens, those fascists out to make a killing - what are they doing? They are furthering the Evil in this world. These people express Evil. And if Evil is an independent force that's using people in order to become more present, then the shape the planet is in suddenly begins to make sense. Maybe, these days, Love no longer is all around, but Evil is. So there's your connection with the Apocalypse.

When I crashed my car, in that deep darkness I felt the presence of something under the surface of life that goes on living with and without us. Not quite Gods, but something God-like. I had the distinct feeling these 'forces' had an interest in my driving around, crashing, and living to tell the tale. Maybe what I felt was the undercurrent of Love and Evil and whatever else is out there looking for us. They did not have an interest in my being happy or sad, except insofar as my feelings enabled them to propagate.

Of course, I realise that this runs contrary to what most people believe. If people are expressing something that really isn't of their own making, this means our actions may not be voluntary, or at least may not be an expression of our own free will. And if there is one thing almost everyone agrees on, it's that we are independent individuals, acting out of our own desires. We tell ourselves we have free choice, because it is only then that our feelings and our actions make sense. To be loving is a choice, and to be evil is a choice as well. What's more, all of us together, and each for themselves alone, feel that we have a Self and a personality. We may be baffled by our own choices at times, we may not understand why we're doing something even while we're doing that whatever-it-is, but, ultimately, we feel our own, individual, private Self drifting on the waters of our own individual, subconscious ocean. When I decided to drive my car in spite of my fatigue, I was the only thing accountable for that choice - or was I?

The notion of free choice is all fine and well, but it does leave us with some very problematic sides of human nature. For one thing, the coming Apocalypse is of our own making. Those fascists gear up to take it out on the immigrants, even when they must know they are not going to benefit by their actions. Politicians let the planet rot knowing full well that millions will suffer. If there aren't any forces acting through us, then why is 'free choice' so great? None of that makes sense. How is it more comforting to think so many people just happen to be evil individuals? How is it in any way a comforting thought that people freely choose to murder and to maim? How is that better and more believable than thinking we are unknowing instruments of mighty forces that want to be expressed? This belief in individuality is not an attractive thought at all, in fact it's downright depressing. On top of that, when you realise that everything in nature is connected, our belief in individuality is very probably wrong. We may be extremely aware of our very own individual feelings, but that does not mean we are in control of what causes these feelings. But then, if we're not in control, then what are we doing?

If none of our actions are truly of our own making, then we're dealing with the contradictory situation whereby we see our societies are wanting, but none of us are the agents that can freely decide to effectuate any kind of change. Therefore, we need to assume that we are individuals with a modicum of control, because, if we don't, we rob ourselves of our very humanity. However, we also need to assume that we are manipulated by certain 'forces', because this enables us to see why seemingly disastrous action is taken or why necessary actions are ignored. All of which leads to the conclusion that there are forces out there that want us to act in good and benevolent ways as well as in less savoury ways, and we, as individuals, can influence these ways.

But then, and this is what I realised, how shall we describe these forces? 'Love' and 'Evil' seem terms that are all too human. These terms are inadequate by their very nature. The forces do not limit themselves to human emotions. We're not the only creatures that express these forces. There are plenty of other animals out there that seem to know what love is, and that indeed express love, except they do it in ways that are very different from ours. It's just the same with evil. Also, there are probably other forces out there, too. Who knows, maybe Anger and Joy, or Sadness. Maybe Consciousness is out in the world as a force, learning from us, in co-dependence with us. It's probably more correct to think of these forces as, well - 'demons', or maybe as 'gods'.

To think of an intangible world that surrounds us as a world of Gods and Demons is traditionally the realm of shamans and priests. And so it is the realm of religion. Now, I'm no shaman, I'm not a guru, and I'm certainly not a priest, but I can see that as a society we need a way to escape from what is happening to us - and that escape can only come about if we allow for the possibility of Gods and Demons. And so, regardless of what that makes me, I offer up a new Faith.

There is a 'Self' in each of us that we can feel, but that Self needs to be taught a lesson. We can escape the egotism and all-out madness of this 21st Century only by finding a new religious awareness while avoiding the trappings of the old. And I believe I have found a way to see what that awareness might look like. I may not be a guru, but I have a Faith to offer that may enable all of us to live the good life.

What I have found is a mythology that enables all of us to open our eyes to a new way of being. What I offer is a way to avoid speeding towards the Apocalypse, and waking up to find that the dark undercurrent that was always there is spilling over into daily life. I propose to forget about the very entertaining notions of woke comedians and un-woke politicians, and to step into a reality that is simply more real than the one we're caught up in. Let's change the world, because the world needs changing. I suggest we forget about love and death, and go save the planet.

Let's begin something new, based on the wisdom of old. Here goes.

A brief history of the world: Where we come from

Out of nothing, the Universe was born. This birth included suns and stars, and planet Earth. In the beginning, Earth was little more than a glowing rock. Rock, water, fire and sky, that's all there was, or so we are told. Miraculously, out of basically nothing came fish, dinosaurs, and people. People huddled together in caves until the dinosaurs conveniently died out so we could start hunting down the fish. Next thing you know, history has become the story of kings and pharaohs, as well as the story of warfare and plunder.

I realise that it's a little more intricate and complicated than this. That's where Google comes in, you can look up the intricacies and complications. The point I'm trying to make is that for a lot of our best and brightest it seems perfectly acceptable to believe it took two miracles to create life out of nothing, and from then on all developments are perfectly logical. Whatever logical gaps remain, Darwin's theory of evolution and the survival of the fittest will help it all make sense. The development of the material world was... inevitable.

However, to my mind, it doesn't make sense, and it never has. I have accepted the theory of evolution, because the alternative seemed to be stories in which a God created a world out of rage or spite, or just for the sake of creating something new. These alternative histories are fun, but they don't actually explain anything, either. Why would a God be interested in creating this blue planet, and for that matter, why be interested in creating people when you have the power to create something as weird and wild as a sabre-tooth tiger or a Pterodactylus?

Admittedly, the creation histories of the world, as told in ancient scriptures, can and probably should be read as metaphors. When doing so, you'll find they all more or less tell the same thing: In the beginning there was nothing, except for Gods bickering amongst themselves. These Gods are in essence forces and phenomena, such as Darkness or Thunder, represented as brutes with desires. Sometimes a God tears himself in half, thus creating the sky from one half and the earth from the other. Other times, the Gods are a mismatched pair of lovers. Creation by a God just because He feels like talking to someone else for a change is another metaphor.

In all these stories though, out of this more-or-less wilful act of creation, people arise, and wo/man-made history begins under the more-or-less active supervision of a single God or a bunch of Gods. In brief, as metaphors, these tales really tell the same thing Science teaches: First there was nothing, and then there was something.

A brief history of the world revisited: How The Consciousness came into being

I hate to say it, but I'll say it anyway: Science isn't so great. As a religion, it's to be preferred over bigotry and prejudice, but as Nietzsche already noted, Science merely describes what is out there in the Universe, then passes it off as an invention. That's not quite true anymore, as scientists have learned to put things together that nature hadn't thought of, like hydrogen bombs, but I'm sure you catch my drift. Science has a methodology and a language, and it sticks by these for better or for worse. So, if you happen to need a language that tries to deal with the metaphysical, Science is no good. You simply cannot use the language of Science to deal with the esoteric, or, you can, but this won't help to put your mind at ease. Nor can you use the language of science to reason yourself out of the dangers Science presents.

At some point - roughly speaking, around the seventeenth Century and the Age of Enlightenment - the notion took hold of the Western world that religious thought should also be expressed in scientific terms. In many ways, this march of progress has resulted in a loss of knowledge. As clerics started to try to prove the existence of God, they succumbed to the lure of a language that is in essence alien to the notion of what Gods are. With this semi-scientific language, Gods disappeared out of sight. The existence of Gods cannot be proven, and one shouldn't even try. We need Gods - and Gods need us, I'll get to that later - not to prove a point, but to make sense of the world we find ourselves in. So forget about Science for a moment, and let's start anew.

A brief history of the world, pt.2.

When the Earth was begotten from the great Mother-Father who stands at the beginning of time, wild spirits swerved among the rocks. As Fire, Earth, Water and Sky lay dormant, these spirits rose up and they swooped down, they were unconscious and blind, thrusting about like leaves in a winter storm. They dove into Fire, sweeping the heat across the waters, making the waters boil and steam. They dug into the Earth, throwing up rocks and lava, creating great valleys and enormous mountains, then covering these very mountains with seas and throwing rocks into the seas just to make the waters splash about. These spirits had no sense of self, no notion of form, they had no limits as there was nothing to be limited by, they just swirled and curved, and the earth was a hopeless place where nothing could ever find a peaceful moment.

As time went by, some of these spirits gained a notion of the consequences of their actions. They would make a glowing rock rise up from a cloud of steam without any effort - you could say, because they themselves were the rocks and they were the steam at that very same moment - and then they would notice the rock suspended in this cloud, and they would find themselves waiting. What were they waiting for? Did they get bored by their own senseless games? Did the rocks and the water play a trick on them? Did something come into being because of fire discovering the sky? Maybe as the spirits merged with each other, they were changed, and then split off into different directions and into different beings. It's clear though, something happened that made the spirits pause, and in that moment they learned to see how they could create things.

Once they had created something, they would leave it as it was, only occasionally touching upon it, and leaving it again. They didn't have any sense of what they had done and why they had created this thing. Then one day, in another great storm of fire and fury, two spirits smashed into each other, and they created something that was unlike anything that had ever been created before. Let's say it looked like a dragon as drawn by an elephant that's having a nightmare. And this thing, whatever it was, had somehow embodied some of these spirits. Inside of this horrible body the spirits thrashed about, trying to get out, but they couldn't. The spirits inside of the body called out to the spirits outside of the body, and for the first time ever, they became aware of their own being. And so they waited. Waiting, they learned that they could learn. And this is how The Consciousness was born.

At first, The Consciousness was not really very aware of anything much. It just existed on the inside of this snake-like Thing as well as on the outside swirling around, wondering what had happened. After a while though, as the spirits within learned how to communicate with the spirits on the outside, something was understood. The snake-like Thing started to move, and while moving, it destroyed and created. There may have been a Consciousness to guide it, but in its physical appearance the snake really was no more than a ragged being, alive yet helpless and dangerous. The spirits on the outside tried to help their imprisoned fellow-spirits, and started to coax the Snake of Chaos to the water. As it tore through the earth, it ripped its flesh on the rocks, and from each fallen bit a new snake would form, and inside every snake some spirits found themselves locked up. Finally, the beasts came to the Ocean, where they swam off in all directions, taking on different forms as they went.

As time went by, the conscious spirits learned to communicate with Chaos. They learned to tell it where to go, and they could tell it what to do. Then they started making more creatures, getting inside of every thing they had created, and they investigated this new way of being. Where they had once thrown rocks into the air, they now tried to eat them or make a building out of them and curl up inside. Where they once made the waters boil, they would now make their creatures shoot out water from their backs. They created little things with thousands of legs that ran through cracks in the rocks and dug deep into the earth, just like the spirits did when they were not inside of a body. Some of the spirits could move in and out, but some others found that once inside a body they were trapped, and so they learned how to make the best of a bad situation. Some of the spirits that were trapped turned mean and sullen, they resented the ones that could still fly through the air freely. Others stayed in close contact with the free-flowing spirits and told stories of how it was to be inside of a body that had four brightly coloured wings covered with eyes, and how it felt to walk on the bark of a tree-spirit.

The world changed because of all of this, and the spirits came to understand that they were different when they were on the inside from what they were on the outside. They had different longings and different needs. The ones that were angry attacked the others and swallowed them, and once inside, the spirits would begin to fight with each other, destroying their creature as they did. When this happened, they would shoot out of the broken body and join the spirits of the air once more. Some spirits manufactured giant monsters, just to be able to attack the others with their creation. They liked this so much that they never stopped, this is how Evil and Anger came into being. Many of the spirits liked to use their bodies to learn new things though, they liked each others company, and this is how Love and Joy took on permanence.

    Still, the Snake of Chaos was always out there in the waters. Sometimes it lay silent for a while, but then it would always try to swim, and when it did so, its wild movements made the oceans rise up and fall down, and the great Snake would fall along with the waters. One day, the Snake landed on an island, and a piece of flesh was torn off by a rock. The giant beast hurled itself back into the sea, bleeding, but somehow the part that was left behind didn't wither and neither did it turn into just another form of Chaos. Inside of it, a spirit was making it take on another shape, something it couldn't conceive of yet. All the other spirits gathered around and they tried to help. Evil said it had to become a big thing with claws and rip the other beings apart. Joy told it to make sure that it could make sounds, and said it would be fun to be bright orange or blue. Love said it needed tentacles with which to hold on to the others. They gave so much advice and they had so many suggestions that the atmosphere all around heated up. The spirit on the inside became frightened, it tried to act on what everyone suggested, it tried to grow tentacles, it tried to look mean - and then it just started to scream. All the spirits fell silent as they watched a soft, warm, naked thing with a skin that had all colours, and with really rather small claws. And this is how mankind was born, lying on a beach, covered with the blood of the Snake of Chaos.

Man walks among us

Just to overstate the obvious: We do not know for certain if the birth of conscious life really happened this way. It probably did, but that's not the point. What matters is that it's no less plausible a story than life evolving out of nothing and it's more fun. Plus, it shows that when talking about life and people, we need recourse to the language of myths. After all, when looking at this world that surrounds us, there are manifestations that boggle the mind. Animals that eat rocks really exist, they're bacteria. There are mammals, namely whales, that shoot steam from their backs. People also exist, and we are complex and confused beings, to say the least. If not for myths, neither our common ancestry nor our intellectual history makes sense. We need myths to give meaning to what cannot be understood. It doesn't matter at all whether you think a mythical story is true in the sense of what-really-happened. What matters is if the story gives you a language to talk about what you feel you are or might conceivably come to be. You need a language to express your needs.

An aspect of our existence that can only be addressed through the language of myths is, simply put, that there is something deeply problematic about being human. After all, as the eminent anthropologist David Graeber noted, there doesn't seem to be any society in which the human condition is not seen as a fundamental problem. The existence of work, sex, and reproduction are all troubling ways of negating the possibility of a good life, as well as human desires always being fickle. Then of course, there's the fact that we're all going to die. So, as Graeber writes, there's a lot to be troubled by.

How come we have so many sensibilities, so many feelings, in fact, so much of everything; and still we seem to be fundamentally unaware of the world we're living in? What is our raison d'etre? Why are we here? Man lets their brief stay on earth be ruled by a handful of armed idiots and sells the very earth itself for the abstraction of money, and then will kill to defend the property of the rich against the onslaught of other poor schmucks just like themselves. It may all make sense to some, but I find it increasingly strange. And when anyone tells me, 'This is how it's always been', or worse still, 'This is the best of all possible worlds,' then I'm inclined to roll my eyes, stick my fingers in my ears, and scream 'LALALA!' at the top of my lungs. I cannot understand how a species as inventive as ours has created societies that are so brutal - least of all when the people you meet tend to be good and helpful.

Darwin is of little use, even though, when thinking of the endless variety of living things coming into being, it is surely possible to agree with him on some of the processes that have taken place. The glowing rock that was the young earth needed to cool down before there could be water, just as there needed to be simple creatures before more complex beings could arise. I will believe all that and I won't be ironic about it, but it doesn't help me understand quite how a Dinosaur is a simpler creature than a cockroach, nor does it help me understand myself. Whereas, when I think of a baby on a beach covered with the blood of the Snake of Chaos, this does actually give me a picture of what I am, and Darwin be damned.

If you're still with me, I'm giving you fair warning, this is where it gets weird. It really is hard to say which is more true: Life springing up out of nothing, because of Science, or some kind of entity that created spirits and those spirits then creating living beings. It's all equally baffling, and it gets stranger still. Even when not letting go completely of scientific reasoning, we still find that there are many things happening in this world that cannot be explained, and although they can be described, the description does not offer much to hold on to. As a quantum-scientist once told me, 'We think we are no longer in Plato's cave staring at shadows on a wall and believing it is the real world we're looking at. However, we're now merely at a stage where we know that we have been looking at shadows on a wall instead of at the real world, but we are still in that same cave.'

By way of an example, consider this. It is accepted in quantum theory that certain connected pairs of particles can be split, with one particle shooting off to the North pole and the other to the South pole, or even one particle shooting off into outer space and the other staying home. However, this splitting off does not sever the connection, and when something happens to the one particle this instantly influences the other particle as well. It doesn't matter how far apart they are, the effect is instantaneous. This is known as 'the spooky connection between particles' - Einstein's phrase - and it has been experimentally proven. No time delay, no atomic bindings that we have any idea off, and yet it happens. This is science, and it's magic at the same time. The particles know something that we don't.

You might ask, 'Well, what do particles know?' And I will answer with a counter-question: 'How can their connection be explained if not in terms of knowledge?' And then you might wonder, 'If there is a connection between two particles over distances of thousands of miles, wouldn't there be many of these connections surrounding us, and if there are, how come we never notice this?' To which

I reply that maybe we do notice the knowledge of particles, but we do not know that we notice. And in fact, I'm inclined to believe it is so. We are subjected to knowledge and forces that we do not know exist and that we have no control over. So why not call these forces 'spirits' instead? Why not accept that our lives may very well be ruled by forces that we need to deal with in a way that we may have once known but have now forgotten?

In a similar vein, what about the idea of Acupuncture and the 'energy lines' running through the body? Even modern medicine has accepted this principle of an 'energetic organisation of the body', but modern medicine cannot explain why it is so. Experienced acupuncture practitioners can work with the phenomenon though, even when it is not known in what way the Chinese doctors once figured this system out. Regardless, there is apparently a system of a connected body-energy, and if it is present in humans, then it is probably present in the bodies of other animals, too, and you can safely assume it will be present in many, if not all, other living shapes in nature. These energy systems are not - in fact: cannot - be separated from the greater world that connects everything. Which is all to say that there are modes of transport of energy that are inside of every individual body and that are similar to the way the other bodies are organised, and all these modes are connected through a greater energetic 'network' that is out in the world. People didn't invent energy, it was there before we came along. So, you may call these energetic systems by any other name, but you might also call them 'spirits', probably without making their mysterious nature any more obscure.

And while I'm at it, if people are ruled by unknown spirits, then, of course, our societies are also the result of these unknown spirits interacting. Societies are human creations, but if humanity is the creation of unknown forces, then society is ultimately the creation of these forces at least as much as it is the creation of humans. I've come to believe that if only we learn how to understand what forces are out there ruling us, 'the good life' is ours for the taking. And because these forces are 'out there' as well as 'in here', we really need to open ourselves up to new learning experiences. It's not just scientific exploration and cold facts that we're after, it's the world of Demons and Gods that we need to investigate.

This all comes dangerously close to trying to reason one's way into religion, I realise that. Using some weird quantum phenomenon to prove the existence of spirits is probably as misguided as trying to find the correct mathematical formula to calculate the amount of angels that fit on a pin. There is a difference, though. What I suggest is simply that we find ourselves in a world that holds great mysteries, and although Science may describe these mysteries, they still remain mysteries. We need to learn once more to accept that the mystery lives inside of us, and is connected to a mystery that lives outside of us. If we find a way to make the mysterious less abstract while not forgetting about its elusive nature, we may come to find a better understanding of the things that give peace of mind. In fact, we may find peace of mind without needing much of anything more.

So, let's assume that when the earth came into being there were spirits, and these spirits have evolved into forces such as 'Love' and 'Evil', 'Joy' and 'Anger'. They live through the endlessly complicated billions of creatures that they have brought into existence, and they communicate with the spirits that are still shapelessly flying through the air and digging into the earth. And always there is the Snake of Chaos growling and snarling, wreaking havoc, and leaving parts of its monstrous body behind as it goes on its way.

In this world of connected particles, snakes and spirits, goes wo/mankind as a driver asleep at the wheel of a car speeding through the night.

Do you believe in magic?

I'm hardly the first to proffer the notion of good or bad spirits exerting their influence on the daily grind. Gods, Demons, and ghosts have been around for a while. Many people are familiar with that most famous spirit known as 'the Holy Ghost', but there are more spirits roaming our world. The awareness of 'something out there in the night' has a respectable pedigree. The explanation for their existence may be either mythical or anthropological, and the truth is that they're probably both.

In 'The testament of Solomon', a text dating back to the 2nd century CE, the story is told of problems while building the greatest temple of all time. In this text, King Solomon is charged with fulfilling the promise his father King David made to the god of the Jews, YHWH. Solomon needed to build a new temple, so that the ark of the covenant could be kept safe for worship.

During construction however, problems arose. At night a demon named Ornias was sucking the life blood out of the main workman. King Solomon asked YHWH for help, and via the angel Michael, the God kindly sent Solomon a ring with a special seal. With this seal, and with the help of an angel named Ouriel, Solomon ordered the demon Ornias to invoke the powerful demon Beelzeboul, who in turn called out all the other demons. Solomon subdued them with his ring, learned their secrets, then put them all to work on the temple. When building was done, the King drove the demons in bottles, which he sealed shut with the mighty ring. You might say, this was 'one ring to rule them all'. Alas, many years later, Babylonians invaded Jerusalem and destroyed the temple. Searching for gold, the Babylonians broke the bottles, and thus let loose upon the world a full army of demons. From then on, people are under constant attack.

The mirror image of this tale is told in the mythology of the Piaroa, a people living along the great river Orinoco in Brazil. Their culture is very peaceful, instead, it's the gods that are in trouble. It is told that Piaroan society was the creation of an evil, cannibalistic god. Their theology tells of endless, invisible wars in which insane, predatory gods cause many deaths. These in turn need to be avenged by the symbolic massacre of whole, unknown, magical communities. So, while the Piaroans are carefully considerate of each other, they are also aware of the destructive madness that lives in the world of the gods. Because of this origin, the people define themselves as caught between a world of the senses and a world of reason. By necessity, learning how to navigate one's way through life involves thoughtful consideration for others, as well as the cultivation of a sense of humour. Keeping a balance between feelings and thoughts is the best way to keep the world of the gods from spilling over into the world of the people.

When considering these two mythologies, you'll notice that they both assume the demon world is always present. The demon world can be represented as a destructive force that has come out of an invisible world and is now an everyday menace in the lives of humans, or it can compel people to be wise and cheerful in order to ensure that the fight is contained in the other world. Whatever the case may be, in order to maintain peace in their own lives, it is up to the people to gain insight into the dangerous ways of gods and demons.

The 'invisible world' is in many ways the shadow of society. Talking about this world can reveal a worldview in which people are ultimately left by the Gods to battle it out on their own, as in the myth of King Solomon, or it can show a worldview where the people need to unite in order to keep the dangerous Gods out, as it is for the Piroans.

When a society has lost the language to talk about the shadow world, this does not mean the invisible world has disappeared, neither as a symbol nor as a reality. All the ungodly lack of conversational skills reveals is that dangerous beliefs have taken the place of constructive symbolism, and conversely, dangerous symbolism has taken the place of constructive beliefs. Taking this realisation into the modern-day world, it becomes clear that we need to find the lost knowledge of an invisible world that either sustains us, or that is out for our destruction. Without that knowledge, our societies are at the mercy of forces we have no control over.

The awful truth

Before diving any deeper into the world of the mysterious, allow me to make some preparatory remarks as to the nature of what we're up against. We need to care about 'our' demons, because as a species, wo/mankind finds itself in a bit of a fix. Or, as a vessel of evil spirits, humanity has come to be used for practices that are violent and destructive at the expense of the good forces.

It was Leonard Cohen who once wrote, 'There is no decent place to stand in a massacre.' And when you look around, you can see we are indeed standing in a massacre, albeit the massacre of the natural world.

A study of insect life in German nature reserves has found that in a little under 30 years more than 70% of insect life has vanished. That study was published in 2017. The rate of extinction of insects is eight times faster than that of mammals, birds and reptiles, but that is not a consolation. Humanity has also wiped out 60% of mammals, birds, fish and reptiles since 1970, a major report produced by the World Wildlife Fund concluded in 2014. The very structure of the natural world, in all its myriad splendour created over billions of years, is coming undone by the human consumption of ever more food and resources. If there was a 60% decline in the human population, that would be equivalent to emptying North America, South America, Africa, Europe, China and Oceania. Presumably, it would be cause for action if that started to happen.

Feeling depressed already? Don't worry, you're not alone. According to the World Health Organization in 2018, depression and anxiety disorders cost the global economy $1tn a year, with a 50% increase in the number of people with depression or anxiety between 1990 and 2013. That statistic in itself is a reason to feel depressed though, because, as you may have noticed, quite why depression is a problem is expressed in terms of money. The global economy suffers because of people, well, what do you know?

The current state of affairs has by and large come about through the troublesome notion of money as a standard to measure reality by. As anyone realises who's ever seen a German postage stamp from the 1920's for 3 million German Reichmarks, or has seen photographs of people pushing a wheel-barrow stacked with money bills, inflation shows that 'money' is not a real thing of any lasting worth. Money is a symbolic representation of a symbolic belief in a symbolic way of living. By this I mean that 'money' is only worth the paper it's printed on, because of an agreement none of us have made to accept the belief that money can buy everything. The ability to buy and sell through the use of symbols in turn leads to everything being up for grabs, there is nothing of inherent value to counteract the trade. Trade in itself has become the over-arching religion.

The belief in money is used to organise a society, even when its symbolic nature leads away from any notion that it may be connected to the happiness of people living lives that are all too real. Money is not at the root of all problems, though. Belief is. The belief in money has facilitated the world trade, thereby enabling industry to spread like a disease, but it's not at the origin of wo/man's appetite for destruction. The thing with people is just that we like to believe stuff. We like to tell each other stories around the campfire, going, 'It's true! I saw frogs raining from the sky with mine own eyes!' - and all that is good fun, until it stops being fun, which is where we're now at.

When you ask most children at the age of five to draw an animal, chances are they will draw an elephant. This is cute, but out in the wild, elephants, like most animals, are hunted to extinction. This wave of extinction has come about through placing a price on animal lives. Their lives are not considered intrinsically valuable - not like human lives - but are given value through the laws of The Marketplace. It is believed the rules of the Marketplace are such that, notwithstanding the animals dying, wealth and property for most people are assured. These assumptions are based on myth, albeit not on a very attractive kind of myth. In this case, the myth is that private property will safeguard individual freedom. Up to a certain point this may be true for some, but the amassment of property obviously has the opposite effect: There is a lot less freedom for most, especially if you happen to be a non-human animal.

Another point that is occasionally mentioned, but rarely believed, is that nobody actually owns anything. Death will come, and neither your body or your soul will take any stuff into the next world. This is nicely illustrated by the ancient Egyptian practice of mummification and burial procedures. The Egyptians of old buried their pharaohs with jewels and other riches, so that they might be wealthy in the next world too. See where that got them. It has merely led to these graves being plundered by robbers or by archeologists in the centuries after.

The belief in money equals a belief in myth. Take the tale I stumbled upon while visiting a museum that was dedicated to the history of money. It concerned a now-lost civilisation on an island in the South Pacific. These people had a currency that consisted of a particular kind of wheel-shaped stone that was produced on another island. The bigger the stone, the more valuable. These stones were transported from the production island to the main island with boats, but every now and then, a boat would be caught up in a storm and sink, sometimes carrying big, valuable stones. These stones could not be recovered. However, all the inhabitants of this society knew of their existence and to whom the stones belonged. Therefore, the stones were not considered 'lost', they remained part of the money system. People continued trading and paying with these stones, except some stones happened to be at the bottom of the ocean. For all practical purposes, you might say these stones had been turned into spirits, whose powers could be transferred from one person to the other. And if you think this is a crazy way to think about the value of currency, just consider our Western belief in electronic payment. We pay for our daily bread with plastic cards that alter the numbers in our bank account and presto! the baker has gotten richer. The numbers are the magic code by which we abide, and they might as well be calculated by a computer at the bottom of the ocean.

Just to avoid setting myself up for scorn, I'm not saying the abstraction of money has not had its uses. The money system has allowed for a more comfortable way of living for a lot of people, I will grant you this. All I'm saying is that this money system has had its day. Money in itself is nothing, so the pursuit of money isn't really worth much either. This belief in money can only be worthwhile if it actually leads all of us into a worthwhile situation.

Because of the belief in the value of money, pretty much everything is for sale. The situation really is rather awful. We, all of us, live in a world of unassailable myths, yet in the real world we no longer have a decent place to stand. In spite of individually being mostly decent and good, we have come together in societies that act in a destructive manner. Obviously - yes, obviously! - there is a necessity to create better societies, and we can only do this if we are aware of our beliefs. I believe a kinder world is what all of us want, and this can be achieved only through fearlessly examining some of the assumptions that have not been helpful thus far, and replacing them with ones that are.

We need to change the world, which is rather a daunting task, but we may start by trying to let go of some of our beliefs. Because, like it or not, the truth is not dependent on your beliefs. There may be convictions you can cling to, but they are not the truth. On the other hand, there is something out there in the world that works its magic on you, and whatever it is, it exists independent of any belief. Still, your actions have consequences, so your beliefs do matter.

Belief is what it's all about. All belief is based on arguments, and if there is argumentation, there is no truth. Truth just is, it doesn't need arguments and beliefs. From this, it follows that the beliefs of people who will buy us all a one-way ticket to the precipice are not the truth. We can't trust these beliefs nor can we trust these people, and instead, we should put our faith in friendship and kindness. Kindness does not need arguments, because all kind acts are true, grace of their very nature.

Also, just so you know, truth doesn't need to be spread by violent means. Truth is not a weapon with which to cut off the heads of your enemies. If something is true, it will be true regardless of what anyone else believes in, and so the mere idea that the truth needs to be furthered through cruel actions is, well, let's say, 'misguided'. When we find some kind of truth, no further belief is needed. When we find a faith that enables a new and kinder way of living, it's perfectly alright to stick with that, and then leave the world of capitalist myth behind.

If wo/mankind is thought of as a completely independent species living off nature in a human-made world, then it's hard to hold on to anything approaching 'hope'. Now is no time to mope though, it's time to consider that old saying: "When the going gets tough, the tough get going." Subsequently, assuming you and I are The Tough, we need to decide on the direction we're planning to take. In order to achieve any meaningful change, better myths need to be found. Through these more attractive myths, a more attractive way of living may be established.

You gotta have Faith

So we need Faith, not belief. We have to change the future of our history, and to that end we have to have Faith. We need to find our bearings again. We need a new Faith, because what we had has failed us. This new Faith will have to offer an alternative to the forces of industrialised society, to loneliness, and to enmity. Finding our way back to such a Faith can be done. Our societies haven't always been like this, and there is no need to think we are inevitably at the mercy of people who will wield their slings and arrows while sending us all on our way to an outrageous fortune. These people are probably being terrorised by demons themselves, so we need to see them for what they are. To be sure, the kind of Faith I propose does not equal another set of beliefs, nor religion, nor dogma. 'Faith' means feeling secure in the knowledge that what you desire is truly good and worthwhile, and your desires will lead you to act in a manner that has the well-being of the entire world at heart. That is what 'Faith' means to my ears.

In a sense, I'd say Faith means having guidelines for following the famous categorical imperative of Immanuel Kant (1724 – 1804). This imperative says that you should at all times act in a way that you wish everyone would act all the time. Therefore, the Faith we need should enable you to adjust your actions according to this imperative. A faith that causes you to act in a way that you wouldn't want all others to act as well is not something to go by.

Having Faith also means that you know what these guidelines for good actions are based on, as well as being able to trust that ultimately, your actions will bring forth happiness and will not cause suffering. This Faith will keep you from acting in a manner that is harsh and cruel, because you know that you would not want to live in a world in which everyone was harsh and cruel all the time.

And, because we are people, we don't just need Faith, but we also need to base our Faith on stories that have deep roots in the mythological origins of the world. We need something that is ancient and strong, something we can hold on to. We need a decent place to stand, and we can find that place only if we know what is decent to begin with. For us to find our place, we need to know where we came from, and how we got to where we are. We need to know where we're heading, as well as how to travel. We need a roadmap to, well, maybe not 'happiness' exactly, but let's say to 'the good life'.

The good life. People used to enjoy it, judging by those brightly coloured photographs from the 1950's and 1960's featuring all those familiar faces. The good life was Jackie Kennedy smiling her broadest smile, and it was Grace Kelly becoming Princess Gracia of Monaco, and it was every family driving a pink Cadillac. Mothers in the kitchen looking glamorous, and couples sipping cocktails. It was there for the taking when every paperboy could become a millionaire and on Saturday night everyone went dancing in their local dance hall. Or, if you happened to be French, you could just get yourself the good life with a baguette and a bottle of plonk out in the country, with your children stashed in the back of a Citroën DS. The Good Life was The Beatles singing 'All You need is Love' on the first world-wide telecast.

The good life, as lived in the good old days, has been and gone. It has been bought and sold, and then it lost its lustre. It was sold to us with the promise of a new golden era of a global market, and then it just evaporated. The good life came hot on the heels of World War II, it was all the rage in 1967, and then it was gone by the time Margaret Thatcher entered the scene in 1975.

'The good life' though, was a materialist fantasy, it was never real. It needed people more than people needed it, and of course it disappeared from sight. There never was a lot of Jackie to go around to begin with, and there were only four Beatles. The others could merely sing along with songs about pink Cadillacs, they could not actually own one. The good life was an image perfected by advertising agencies. Still, the fantasy was attractive enough, so why couldn't it become a reality? Why did the fantasy ever fade?

I humbly offer two explanations.

The first deals with the principles underlying a globalised, capitalist system. The basic promise of globalisation is that of efficient corporations competing for the consumer's money by offering the best products at the lowest prices. Even at the level of common sense, this idea is obviously flawed. Inevitably, the 'most efficient' corporation will drive production costs down by using the cheapest materials possible and offering wages just above the point where workers will go on strike or otherwise become unproductive. Getting the cheapest materials possible leads to disregard of the environment, and paying the lowest wages acceptable leads to a semi-permanent moving of production facilities to countries with ever-lower wages. Meanwhile, governments trying to create job security for their population will compete with other countries by offering the lowest possible tax rates to the very corporations that will hardly pay their workers. When wages are at their lowest and corporate taxes are all but abolished, the last resort for governments to tempt corporations to stay in their respective countries, is offering the best possible social and physical infrastructure. Both kinds of infrastructure cost money, and so governments are driven into debt. Finally, social unrest will be contained through a combination of an ever expanding surveillance state and brute force. Rampant capitalism ushers in a new age of feudalism, with kings of industry running countries and the people reduced to the status of serfs and slaves.

My second explanation of how the fantasy of the good life has been put on the proverbial back burner goes something like this: Globalisation can only function to the people's benefit if and when the governments of various countries decide that unfettered capitalism is a dead end street. Instead of thinking about what corporations need, governments need to think about what people need. People need an education, food, a clean living environment, sex, drugs, a safe place for the night, and they need to be nursed when they're ill of health. Finally, when the time has come, they need a dignified way of leaving this world behind. On top of that, they need a common, benign culture, an awareness of history and yes, a moral compass. All this runs contrary to the idea of a highly individualised society in which private property is sacred.

I'm not suggesting that the lion shall sleep with the lamb if only industry, money and private property are abolished. I may be a fool, but I'm not that big of a fool. However, what I do suggest is that 'The Economy' is shorthand for a present-day ideology that in essence needs destruction in order to sustain itself. You simply cannot have constant production of consumer goods at ever lower prices without someone or something somewhere suffering. Capitalism, such as we understand it, needs the occasional war. From time to time everything needs to be bombed to smithereens, so that the whole thing can begin again. Weapons are consumer goods as well, let's face it.

Now, bear with me for a bit. All that once was solid dissolving into air may be an inevitable side-effect of a capitalist economy, but creation and destruction are not actually a capitalist invention. In Indian philosophy some 4,000 years ago, there already is the concept of 'the great breath of Brahma'. Brahma being, roughly speaking, the Ultimate Source of All, which creates and destroys worlds in a cyclical rhythm. Brahma breathes out and the universe is manifested. With an intake of breath the universe is called back to the source and ceases to exist, but on breathing out again manifestation begins anew.

Brahma is obviously not an ideology, it is a principle of what might be thought of as 'the reality of the origin'. According to this principle, the Universe is a beginning that is connected to an end that is connected to a beginning. The Universe is a snake forever chasing and catching its own tail, if you will. In this way, creation and destruction are inevitably linked, they will occur time and again, and out of destruction something new will always arise.

So, instead of looking how to 'fix' the economy, as a society, we could decide that destruction may come about, because it inevitably does. The Phoenix will forever rise out of its ashes, possibly leaving dinosaurs and people in its wake, and so be it. There is no need to hold on to anything, because there really isn't anything to hold on to, given that Brahma is the creator as well as the destroyer of worlds, and this Principle will do what it does. But, instead of leaving the destruction to Brahma, we might as well do the work ourselves. In that case, at least we have a choice. We can allow for global capitalism to murder us all in a horrible way, leaving our once-blue planet to those rock-eating bacteria, or we can change things around, and decide to go in another direction. We might just say, 'Brahma breathes in, and a predatory industry comes to a halt. Brahma breathes out, and a kinder way of living is born.'

So, once more, how to find The Good Life?

Epicurus the prophet, or We don't need this fascist groove thang

'Brothers! Sisters! We don't need this fascist groove thang' is a song by British band 'Heaven 17'. They were a funky little outfit, and they wore their politics on their respective sleeves. It's a fitting title, because I am fully aware that the fruits of any kind of organised ideology carry the bad seeds of 'True Faith' inside. True Faith will probably lead to fascism before you have had time to blink your eye. Not to put too fine a point on it, but the siren song of fascism can be heard whenever people get together to decry the actions of other people. Apparently, there is a certain satisfaction to be had in pointing out how others are the enemy. We enjoy pointing out how they're not just mistaken, they are positively bad people, harbingers of doom, and we need to do it to them before they do it to us! In brief, I believe none of us are impervious to the chants of fascism by whatever name it may be called. And thus, the Good Life is not to be found in any True Faith or ideology that pits people against each other. The Faith that I propose will not further antagonism, instead, it will further friendship and kindness.

To illustrate this latter point, I suggest that you, dear reader, now imagine a temple in a clearing in a forest. Imagine you are sitting in the grass, the sun is out, and a pleasant breeze keeps you cool. You are in the company of friends and lovers. Children are playing somewhere off in the distance, you can hear their giggles. A sheep is grazing. Birds are singing high up in the trees. You have enough food - that is, fresh bread and maybe some olives - and you are talking with your friends about what makes up the good life.

Someone says friendship is by far the most important, another says it's wisdom. You say: 'It's our appreciation of happiness that makes for the good life, because with happiness we have everything and without it we are endlessly searching for it.'

'Sure,' someone says, 'But what is happiness, how can you define it?' And you go, 'Well, happiness has no fixed shape, she arises from the study of what gives a life meaning. Of those things, the most important is the belief that the Godhead is an immortal and many-shaped being. The Godhead lets itself be known through the Gods that carry the visible and the invisible worlds. Also, it is not hard to see that there are Gods, because the experience of them is abundantly clear.'

When another of your friends then interjects that you make it seem as though the happiness of people is solely in the hands of the Gods, but, because it is always up to us to decide who we are, aren't we, each of us alone, therefore responsible for our own happiness instead? - that's when you say: 'Yes, we are responsible for our own happiness. One cannot hide behind the will of the Gods, because that will is unknowable to us. However, what each person does for themselves has consequences for that person and for the environment around them. The Gods lead our way, but through our actions we change how the Gods see us and we set an example to others how they can be seen. The idea that people are subjected to unknown forces gives them an excuse to behave as they like, and clearly, they ought not to.'

Now imagine there is a brief pause while your companions are digesting your words, or maybe they just want to take another piece of bread. You think, 'Well, maybe I wasn't clear in what I meant, let's phrase it differently.'

You continue: 'The goal of all our pursuits is to be released from pain and fear, and once we have attained that, the storm in our hearts will quiet. When we have brought about a situation in which everyone can find this kind of peace, then there is no longer any cause to seek out anything else. That is why we do not blindly chase after every pleasure. Oftentimes, we forget about something pleasurable, because it will ultimately lead to a greater loss. Also, we undergo torments and endure them for long periods of time, provided their ultimate result is a greater wellbeing. So, just because all that brings wellbeing is naturally good, we still don't have to chase after it, just as all pain is torment, but not all pain is to be avoided. Sometimes we regard something good as an evil and we regard an evil as something good. By measuring the one against the other, the comfort against the discomfort, we arrive at a sensible judgement.'

Suddenly, a stranger who has been listening in, joins the conversation, and she asks: 'There are many delightful things in the world that bring pleasure and cause no pain. Some people live in big houses with golden bathtubs, others spend their money on soft cushions and sweet meals. Are they not free to do so? Do you reproach those that spend their lives in opulence that they seek opulence? Is it not the mark of the happy that they can live in great prosperity?'

That is not quite the reaction you imagined, but you're no fool, so with a nod to the great Indian epic The Bhagavad Gita, you answer: 'If a person lingers on the world of outward appearances, they will be attracted to these; the attraction becomes greed, and greed leads to frenzy. From frenzy arises only caprice, which leads to memory loss, making a clear judgement impossible. This way, man wilts prematurely amidst opulence, and does not see how he has wronged his fellow man or woman.

'Surely, some are very attached to power and gold. They allow themselves to be misled by the ornate promises of merchants, they glorify the world of matter and say: There is nothing better than this. Their minds are consumed by thoughts of wealth and personal gain, they consult only with their avarice, and keep on thinking of new ways to ensure their own possessions and power. The result is discontent and fragmentation.

'Just as a ship is helplessly carried away by a storm, so discernment is dragged off by the greedy mind. Only if the intellect remains unperturbed and allows itself to be led by thoughts of the return to the Godhead can there be peace. For those who see the truth, the world of objects loses its lustre. A sensible person can let go of their desires while still remaining in the world, not lusting after outward appearances, and not weakened by a lack of substance.

'Independence from externalities is a great good not because there should always be scarcity, but because it is better to be satisfied with little. Moreover, that which is natural is easily attained, while vain and worthless things come at great costs. Those who need not suffer hunger, thirst or cold, and can trust that circumstances will remain thus, can vie with anyone in happiness. Wellbeing is not a succession of drinking sprees, not the consumption of tasty fish, the delicate joys of a luxurious table, nor life amidst precious metals. It is calm reason that is used to approach every like and dislike, it is the renunciation of convictions that make the heart bitter.

'The wise believes that there is no good or evil that is caused by change. There is endless good and evil in the world, yet the adversity a sensible person sometimes experiences is preferable to the prosperity that happens to a fool. It is best if our own actions are not dependent on happy or unhappy coincidences. The destiny some talk of endlessly is less important than how we live and what we do. Fate is capricious, but what we do ourselves is never random and we will always justly profit by it or suffer from it.'

And then someone asks: 'How can one still expect happiness in a world where so many people fight each other?'

You think about this for a bit. Then you answer: 'People often think that they are limited by the world and by the convictions of others, but they themselves are the ones that set the limitations. Those in whom desire flows like water in the ocean, endlessly moving yet always the same, will achieve peace. By overcoming adversity and helping our fellows bear their fate, by not despairing at unexpected turns and not hesitating to turn evil into goodness, we show our true nature.

'Do not believe that the future is fixed, do not despair that the future is uncertain. The future is neither entirely dependent upon us, nor is it entirely independent from us. Focus your attention on your good labour not on its fruits. Let attachment go and regard success as equal to failure, without suffering from a lack of vigour. Transcend contradictions and direct your attention to the Heart at the centre.

'Practice these and similar convictions, both in solitude and in the company of kindred spirits, and you will be free amidst the people. The greatest blessing originates from the immortal blessings of the Gods and these blessings are everywhere. Once someone has truly learned this knowledge, they will be at peace, even in the darkest hour,' - then you take another olive, you spit out its pip, and you stare off into the distance. You're probably rather pleased with yourself.

So, imagine you've had this conversation. If so, you've more or less taken the view of the Greek philosopher Epicurus (341–270 BC). Faith does not equal 'True Faith', it equals a healthy detachment instead. What this means is that you, reader, now have a bit of a tool with which to ward off any fascist inclinations. Not just that, you also have an inkling of what the good life might consist of. It's not so bad in the promised land, sitting in the grass with friends, or baking a bread and thinking of how you will share that fresh bread later on in the afternoon.

In any case, I'd think it's far more attractive to believe you might strive for friendship and kindness than to believe this world is made up of enemies and glimmering things.

Obviously, you have to believe in something, or otherwise you won't be able to stand up to the ones whose convictions are dangerous and nasty. But then, if your beliefs do not also show an alternative way to happiness, they won't be able to sustain you through hard times. I think Epicurus should be considered a prophet, and in the Faith that I propose, he is just that. He had a good thing going, and we can all groove along.

We need to talk about Gods

Why should the good life not come about without Gods? Wouldn't it be better to just stick with what we know, and with what we can actually perceive? Why should we conjure up some vague beings that we have no way of getting to grips with? And what's more, why should anyone wish to have faith in Gods when we have enough trouble just with humanity as it is?

I'm inclined to say, 'Because there are also Demons, and everything that is has its opposite. Sure as night follows day and earth is not sky, so Demons will be counteracted by Gods.' I realise my answer might not be fully satisfactory though, so I'll expand on this a little.

At the beginning of time something came into being that has led to the Universe, including the Earth, and, ultimately, to all living beings. Let's call it 'the Life Force'. Because new life is created everyday, it's quite clear the Life Force is still out there. As people, we may be able to murder most of its current manifestations at an alarming rate, but it's highly unlikely that we will be able to murder the Life Force itself. If anything, mankind will go the way of the dinosaur, and in a few million years from now, some other creatures will dig up our bones and turn them into flutes.

The Life Force is a 'God', regardless of the name. The Life Force is Brahma, it is The Supreme Mind, it is The Source, The All, the Unmovable Mover, the Great Beautician In The Sky. The Life Force is the very being that weaves the tapestry of this world, as well as of any other world. Not only is this 'being' at the basis of our world, it is also what makes up the world, it is, in fact, the spooky connection between particles as well as the particles themselves. It is the bond between The Nameless and The Name.

We, people, stare this thing in the face wherever we go. The Life Force is in the act of creating Consciousness, and to this end it needs to manifest. For all we might imagine, we are a manifestation of the Life Force looking at itself. Obviously, if we are a manifestation of the Life Force, then so are all the other living beings, and so are the shells of crabs and the pearls of oysters. Earth, water, fire and sky, they are all manifestations of the Life Force. What this means is that the Life Force is a many-splendored thing, and so it probably has also taken on shapes and forms that humans cannot begin to imagine. These shapes might conceivably be called 'demons' or 'gods', or 'spirits', or 'particles', or 'fields', and anything else you can come up with. What matters is that these unknown and unknowable forms are still in the act of creation, or at the very least, they are in the act of becoming new, hitherto unseen manifestations. As they come into being, in fact, as they are themselves being, they shape the world all around us and we feel this is happening, even when we cannot put a name to this mysterious manifestation of the invisible.

The Life Force probably doesn't care for us so very much, which is not to say we shouldn't care for The Life Force. The Life Force is clearly influenced by the actions of the living beings, because, as far as we know, life on Earth has changed dramatically since the beginning. Even as you read this, incredible changes are happening. So the Life Force may not be interested in us as such, but it may have an interest in what we do, because through our actions change is effected. These changes are not only taking place in the visible realm, i.e. in nature, but they are also taking place in the invisible realm - that is, in the realm of the senses and the intellect.

Of course, this is where it gets really rather complicated: If people are a manifestation of the Life Force, are we all then, in reality, one God in various shapes in the process of understanding the Divine? Are all of us the Life Force manifesting as Einstein trying to figure out that spooky connection? Are people, in fact, the very same Gods and Demons that conceivably live outside of us as well? And if we are, what conclusions can we - or should we - draw from that?

I believe we need Gods, for the same reason that we need each other and that we need a liveable planet. The reason being that we can only come to live The Good Life when we act in accordance with the Life Force - and the Life Force is in a continual process of learning, understanding, creating, and changing. To the Life Force it may not matter so much what it learns, but to us it most surely does. Who knows, maybe the Life Force is in the process of getting rid of all of us. And so, we need a language to talk about Gods in order to understand where we are, who we are, what we are doing, what we are influenced by, and how we shall adjust our actions.

When you think of yourself as living in the world of Gods, and indeed, as a being that the Gods hold an interest in, then your life makes sense. People are not gods, yet it is only when we talk about Gods that we can talk about ourselves. Living in a world of Gods and Demons, we can see we have a task, not just a day job. Without Gods, we are forever ships lost at sea about to be devoured by the Snake of Chaos.

The language of The Faith

The French philosopher Georges Bataille once said that 'Religion is the search for a lost intimacy'. I find that an interesting notion, as it implies a longing for a kind of connection which cannot be expressed through words. After all, what is 'intimacy'? - we know it when we feel it, but words can only point towards intimacy, they cannot be the feeling. On the other hand, if we do not have a language, feelings can't be shared. If we want to connect to the world of the mysterious, as people, we need a language that is at once intimate and open. We connect to the mysterious as well as to the intimacy of each other through a language that is of the tongue and of the heart.

Stories of a mythological origin of 'the greater world' enable talking about this feeling of something divine that is reaching out to connect with the world of people. Meditating on 'The Life Force' can create a comforting sense of intimacy with the unknown. So, let's get to it. Let's talk about the world of the Gods and thus create this language. Reach out and touch The Life Force's hand, to paraphrase Diana Ross.

You might think of the following as a prequel to the story of the Snake of Chaos and a sequel to the origin of people, except this tale isn't meant to be light-hearted and good fun. It is meant to show the outlines of that language with which to reconnect with our longing for a nameless intimacy.

Before we begin, let's agree that 'The Life Force' isn't much of a name to address an ultimate being by. Instead, I'll go with 'The Unity'. Here's what happened at the beginning of times, when the Universe came into existence.

The Unity was a flowing ocean of darkness, which unfolded like a flower. She became The Light. The light was the First one. Out of the First came forth two Gods: one was Beauty, the other was Desire. Out of Beauty and Desire came forth: earth, water, fire, and sky.

Earth, water, fire, and sky, they are material and tangible, they give, they take. They feel all, they give all, they take all. The four are the eternal children. They are the visible world.

Beauty and Desire are like two streams flowing into one. From the one stream comes all that lives: the people and the beasts and the trees and all that dies and is resurrected. All that lives, lives in the light of the First, swims in the stream, and returns to the water when the time has come. The stream is the invisible world.

Earth, water, fire, and sky, and all that lives and all that is, all is connected to the two Gods and they are connected to the First. This covenant is from time immemorial, it has always been and it will always be. When the Gods come together, the First becomes visible. The First is all that lives and dies and is eternal, She gives what She has received, She receives what She will give, She is at perfect peace.

She is the Supreme Mind, a mind that will come, to which all flesh shall go. And when all that lives and all that is shall have gone there, a greater light will be visible, and in this light every shard, every drop and every heart will be as a light. The Supreme Mind will close like a gate and She will be all there is. The emptiness will be more empty still and yet fulfilled with a well-being so great that all the cosmos will be in there. And all that lives and all that is, will have its sign there and every sign shall be visible and connected to The Unity.

A bit of a myth

The Unity opened her eyes, and from her eyes stars flocked like birds. She breathed out, and her breath became the sun, a shining light that went from her and took a place amidst the stars.

She opened her left hand, in which She had held the moon. She opened her right hand, in which She had held the earth. And from her left side She created a daughter, Eleima. She presented the earth to her. From her right side She created a son, Kelaino. She presented the moon to him.

The Unity took the earth and there she created fiery mountains and with her hands she filled the valleys with the waters of infinity. From water and fire she created trees and shrubbery, all the plants, all the animals on the land and all the animals at sea.

To the Goddess Eleima she said: I give you the earth, and I ask that you will remember me in all you do. Remember me in the trees and in the plants, in the animals on the land and in the beasts at sea. I give you these, so that they may serve you, and those that serve you are a part of me and I will remember them at the time of return.

To the God Kelaino she said: I give you the moon as an instrument, so that you may guard over your sister, and show her the light until the end of time, when we will all be together again. However, the God beheld the moon he had been given and complained bitterly. What is this infertile land? he said. It is as a mirror that shows nothing and merely reflects the light, this barren land is like dust between the stars, dust piled on dust. Where are my mountains, where are my valleys? Where are the rivers to replenish the thirsty?

The Unity heard him and said: I gave the earth to your sister to guard over, I gave you the moon and you were charged to help your sister with her task. The moon is a mirror that shines eternally. Control her and serve your sister. Let the light shine where it is needed. Take the water that is on the earth and wash the earth, do not let the living beings dwell in dust and drought, help all that lives and all that is to find their way to the Love and the Beauty. Stand at your sister's side whatever she may do, and in your vigil I will be visible.

The Unity overflowed with love for the Goddess Eleima, and in the midst of all that was alive, she placed people so that they could help her care for the abundance that was all around. Then Eleima created daughters, and in the hearts of the people they made an altar to honour The Unity. And the Goddess spoke to her daughters: Be a guide to the people and do not let them go astray. Lead all people back to their destination, where they shall be at one with The Unity, the eternal Mother-Father.

The Moon God fell silent and seemed humble, but in his heart he felt resentful. He watched the people on the earth and how they worshipped the Goddess and thus honoured the Unity in all that they did. He watched the daughters of Eleima as they guided the people towards the Unity, he saw the happiness that was in returning to Her. And he made himself sons, and he spoke to them: Make your bed with the people, at the feet of the daughters. Show the daughters of the Goddess the beauty of my mirror. Make new desirable things on this earth. Reflect the light and illuminate all that the people shall lose once they've reached their destination. Lament what they have desired and shall leave behind, so that they will not want to listen to their guides and go on eternally. Turn their hearts from the desire of returning, show them the Beauty and show them the Love, but never at the same time, so that they will want to go ever onwards. And in their restless wandering they will not serve my sister but they will be my servants only.

The Unity knew the jealousy of Kelaino the Moon God, and she knew the goodness of the Earth Goddess, and she spoke: I am the beginning and the ending, I am the ocean in which everything finds its destination. In all that people do they shall find me as they do find you. The Heart, in which I am present, will always return to me. The daughters of the Goddess and the sons of the God are loved by me equally, and the sons shall serve me same as the daughters shall. At the altars the daughters have erected in the people, I place the blood of my Heart, and the sons will show how I am visible in every drop. The people will be the messengers between you. As the daughters will help the people return to the Source, the sons will show the ways the people may go. And at the end of times all the sons and all the daughters will return to where I am. At the end of times all blood shall return to the Source, and when we are all one, at the end of time, there will be peace at the centre.

People

So now we have a Godhead and two Gods, the earth has been created, beasts abound. We have conflict, and the potential for drama. Besides, we have people, but they're not very well-defined yet. As I noted before though, if we're going to talk about Gods, we also need to talk about people.

Something like this: Wo/Man is a body that thinks. Thought makes the body small, the body thinks the mind infinite. In the confinement of the body, Wo/Mankind thinks itself the centre of the world. But the world of people is not the world of the Gods, the people are in-between. The people are of the Gods, they come from them and they return to them, but they are not Gods.

The body thinks the thinking. Body and mind are one and learn from each other. The body is the gate to the place where thoughts are made. Thinking is like a fire that burns ever brighter. The body has ignited the fire and will not extinguish it. Those who hear and judge the thoughts, are the same ones that cannot ignore the thoughts. The thoughts are themselves until they part for the return to The Unity.

The undying and unmovable Heart lives where the body lives, but she is not the body.

She is the water that shall return to the ocean. The Eternal Heart shows what is great and will always be great. The Heart is of The Unity, she comes from Her, returns to Her, and will part from Her again. The Heart will live, it won't ever not live.

The Eternal Heart always returns to the Perfection, even when she makes the body her home. In her shall be Beauty and Desire.

What are we talking about here?

When I ran my car into the crash barrier that fatal night, I felt something stirring in the dark. Then, as I was propelled into a disastrous love affair, I was struck by how little sense my pursuits seemed to make, or, for that matter, how little sense life in general seemed to make. I saw how people are fighting, shouting abuse at one another, or actual physical fighting with people getting wounded and maimed. I used to like movies, but even for entertainment, what was on offer was mostly the spectacle of violence. I was awed by how a callous few take everyone's money, and manage to convince the poor that this is the way it should be. I was thinking how tourists circle the globe, while the oceans are emptied out. And as I was thinking about this state we're in, I felt myself slip into despair. I was wondering what happens to a society in which rivers of blood are made to flow by the greed of a few and the convictions of many. It seemed to me that at some point in history we have lost sight of something. And I wondered what that 'something' might be?

I thought of a line out of T.S. Eliot's epic poem, 'The Wasteland': "Who is the third who walks always beside you? When I count, there are only you and I together, but when I look ahead there is always another one walking beside you. I do not know whether a man or a woman." I couldn't remember what lines followed after that, so in my own clunky way I just more or less made something up: "What are these sounds, so that in the midst of night, the house sighs and you hear the clouds move? Why do you feel like singing when at the same time you feel your heart sink? Why is there something and not nothing?"

Then I thought, what does it mean that there is something, and that there is an order to that 'something'? What is that 'man or woman' keeping us company through our lives? Scientists may one day be able to tell us how they think the cosmos is organised, but when you ask, 'What has organised the cosmos?', trying to answer that question inevitably leads to an originator. After all, to think no one has organised this, and it's all merely a fantastic coincidence, seems just as far-fetched and a lot less interesting. Besides, if it's all just coincidence and science, then our lives mean nothing. If we live these lives because we just happen to be here, then everything is allowed, and if everything is allowed, then nothing is of any value.

However, when you ask, 'Why is there something and not nothing?', and when you think, 'Well, maybe there is an originator, and it's not all coincidence, and our lives have a meaning that goes beyond our individual experience' - then a door opens that leads to a way out of the madness. That door opening is what I saw as I was speeding through the darkness.

I was thinking: At some point this Universe came into existence. Let's assume that first there was nothing, and then there was something. Obviously, a change happened in-between, when from nothing came something. In that moment between nothing and something a Godhead came into being. That Godhead is 'The Unity'.

The Unity has opened up and materialised into the visible world, the body of the Godhead became the Universe. At that same moment when time began, the mind of this Godhead transformed into the invisible world, which we'll call 'The Cosmic Awareness'. Or, you might imagine the material manifestation of the Godhead as the God Kelaino, and the invisible manifestation as the Goddess Eleima.

To the Godhead this act of transformation was as mysterious as it is to us. So from then on, She has been gathering information from the ever fragmenting Universe. We, the living beings, supply the Godhead with information. All the people on this earth are messengers, and our actions are the messages the Godhead receives. This means, when we ask the question, 'Why is there something and not nothing?', the answer is: There is something, because the Godhead we call the Unity is the organising principle of the Universe materialising in order to be able to learn. This Principle - that is, the Godhead - is in the process of coming to an understanding, and this is what we notice. So now we have to decide: Do we want this Godhead to be informed about greed and despair, about violence and destruction? Do we want to inform the Godhead about the way we are ruining her planet? Or would it be a better idea to inform the Godhead on the notion of goodness?

Of course, you might think, 'There aren't any Gods,' or 'How can I know if there is this Godhead?' And the answer to that is that, obviously, there is something, and the actions of the living things send out information, and this information brings about a change. You can see this all around you. Not just the big changes are important, the small things matter as well. For instance, when you squash a fly just because it's buzzing around your house and just because you can, then you send out a message of death and destruction. I'm sure we have all at times felt the presence of something evil just before performing such a small act of needless violence. In those moments, we all felt we were informing something out there or, instead, we felt how that very something put us up to acting in a way we did not really want to, but we did it anyway. That message changed the world around you, and it showed the world around you in what way it could be changed.

Therefore, if you accept that you are what makes up this universe and if you accept that there is a Godhead that is learning from your experiences, then it matters that you, too, are connected to the other things that are out there. It matters how you connect to the Earth, to the other living things, to the things that are not living and not dead. It matters how you view the wealth and how you regard the beauty, it matters how you listen to the voices that are out there, it matters how you treat your fellow beings. Most of all, it matters whether you supply the Godhead with information on how violent and destructive people can be, or if you send out messages of kindness, courage and wisdom. It matters if you swat a fly.

So why is there something and not nothing? The answer is: Because there is this Godhead we call 'The Unity', and She wants to know what She can be, and in order to learn about Herself, She needs to know who you are. You are what you inform the Godhead upon.

Out there in the darkness, there is a world of Gods and Demons, learning. There is a Godhead, and She is reaching out, trying to connect to you. This is the Third that always walks beside you. This is why there are these sounds, so that in the midst of night the floorboards creak, and you hear your neighbours sing. This is why you feel like singing even when all too often you feel your heart sink. This is why we, as people, need to re-think the how and why of it all. This is why we need to change the way society is organised, so that the evil gets dispelled. After all, there is something and not nothing, and so we must inform the Godhead of the many ways in which we can make the rivers of Desire and Beauty flow.

The Eternal Heart

The Eternal Heart is what some people would call 'the soul', 'Atman', or 'the essence' of a person. In some heretic Christian teachings it is the divine knowledge that is present in every individual, imprisoned in the body. Let's say The Eternal Heart is the Life Force such as it has taken shape in each of us, and such as it will take shape in some other form of being when the individual body has returned to the earth.

The Eternal Heart is the 'Self beyond the Self'. When you're alone and you're not quite sure what you are, when you are in company and you hear yourself saying things that you hadn't thought of before, indeed, when you are thinking of what happens to you after having shuffled off this mortal coil - that is when the Eternal Heart shows its existence in you. You are connected to the world of the visible and the invisible, not by means of your body or your thoughts, but by means of this Presence that lives within you, yet independent from you.

By comparison, in Buddhist teachings there is the notion of 'enlightenment'. Briefly put, and paraphrased beyond recognition, in the state of enlightenment, there is a complete understanding of the way in which the temporal human condition is wedded to the eternal world of The Supreme Mind. This state of enlightenment is what the Eternal Heart is at all times: It is the connection between the materialisation of the Divine and the immaterial being of the Divine.

The Faith shows a way out of the madness

What haunts me is how it is that people have become strangers among strangers. Why is this life such a lonesome struggle at times?

Society teaches us we're all separate individuals. The ultimate consequence of individualism is the notion that so-called treasures can be accumulated by individuals, and subsequently individuals can band together in armies and fight over possession of these treasures. You can see this all around you, and if you wouldn't know any better, you might believe that humans enjoy feeling separated. You might believe they enjoy the separation between body and mind, between what is and what is not, and between those who 'have it all' and those who live in abject poverty. And then you might say, 'What does it matter that we're all connected, if in practice we spend our time fighting over possession of treasures, and then we die?'

My point of view is that many societies are organised in a way that is wrong. In fact, the way most societies are organised is contrary to how we want it to be. People, like all living things, are in and of the earth, the earth is in and of the Universe, and therefore each of us is just another way the Universe takes shape. We are particles living inside of a Universe that consists of the material world and the invisible world.

The Universe cannot intend to fight itself. If we stop believing we are by our very nature antagonistic, we can experience many different dimensions of the invisible world. We are not separated from each other, and in fact, we're not separated from anything at all. We are not strangers among strangers, nor are we enemies living in the material world. We are merely fragments of the Universe who haven't been introduced to each other yet.

People all over the world may be divided into oppositional groups, but that opposition is not what we enjoy at all. What is keeping us from living a full life is our faulty sense of a unique consciousness. Because of our dogmatic belief that we are unique individuals, we deny ourselves the joy of having all manner of wonderful and amazing adventures of the body and of the mind, or, more precisely, adventures of all the bodies and of all the minds. Just because for so long we have known division and we have struggled so much, the division does not constitute a good way of being. This antagonistic organisation of society is madness.

There is madness all around, but there is no need to assume the madness is inevitable. It's a matter of belief. We can believe we are solitary creatures, endowed with a unique consciousness and a unique sense of self, and then, as a consequence, we each live in our own world with our own individual sense of loss and isolation. We can believe people by necessity are organised as groups in opposition to other groups, separated through desires and needs, and then, as a consequence, these groups of people will always fight over scarce resources and they are eternally locked in battle. In that worldview, life is still brutish and nasty, and it will always be that way.

However, I choose to believe this society of institutionalised solitude is a mistake. It is nothing more than an experiment instigated by a Godhead that just wants to see what's happening. The Godhead can't stop it, because She is not a person - She is the Consciousness that surrounds us and that is trying to become more conscious. We are the ones that have to stop this process.

It's really quite simple. People are a part of the Universe and our actions cause changes in the visible and in the invisible realm. These actions in themselves are neither good nor bad, but the result may be suffering or happiness. Our actions are messages, and we are messengers to the Gods. Upon receiving our messages the Consciousness of the Godhead changes, and then we notice that something has changed. The Godhead has learned from our messages, and the God of the Material World and the Goddess of the Invisible World make us feel what The Godhead has learned. People are not Gods and we can't begin to imagine the way a Godhead incorporates the information given. In this fundamental lack of knowledge lies our agency. We are messengers, who get to decide on the information written in these messages.

Every message contains information about the kind of world each one of us is creating at every moment. This human society of the exploitation of violence, of the constant threat of violence and of actual violence - this society is what people have created and so we might as well create something else. Why should we continue to suffer by our own hands? Our actions may also cause happiness, after all.

In order to get out of the madness, we need to see it for what it is. The madness is the logical extension of the belief that we are in opposition to one another. The madness is at the root of the belief that the material world can be owned by some group, or by some individual. The madness is sustained through those beliefs. However, we are free to take a different path. When you think of people as being essentially all one, and when you think of all of us as living in a variety of worlds that we do not know at all; when you think of animals as fragments in which the universe manifests itself - then you can see that any belief is insane if it causes these fragments of the Universe to seek each other's unhappiness. Just because so many people are led to believe that madness is an everyday fact, this doesn't mean it is so, and it certainly doesn't mean we can't change the madness around.

This being here on earth, being alive, is a mystery to us. So, we need to step out of the madness that is called reality, and fly into the mystery. While you're here, alive in this human shape, you need to explore the mystery. The mystery lies where we let go of our belief of being cut-off individuals. The mystery shows itself when we let go of the belief that we are groups in opposition. The mystery lies where we trust that we can just be here on this earth and sustain ourselves throughout our short lives. When our lives are done, we will return to the Supreme Mind in some other shape or form, and although that is almost as much of a mystery, it's good.

Other people's belief in madness is no reason to stop trusting your own belief in sanity. To the perpetuators of the madness, we are the crazy ones, but we know we are not. We have an idea about where we come from and where we are heading. The Faith that I have sketched out so far shows the way into the mystery - the mystery that lies beyond the madness - and that is where we aim our gaze. We can fly into the mystery and then come back here, and see things anew. Without connection to the mystery of the Gods, there can be no sanity. And it is up to us to create sanity through establishing the ways to connect. It is up to us to find a perfect balance between the material world and the invisible world. It is up to us to find a place where we are completely human, as well as completely at one with the Universe and the Life Force.

Therefore, you can hang on to your sense of Self, while you accept that your Self is as big as the Universe. At the same time, you can let go of whatever it is you believe in, because each of us is merely a fragment, and there is nothing that divides us. We are not strangers among strangers. If sometimes each of us feels alone, that is not because we are alone, it is because we perceive of our own sanity in a world that has gone mad.

The madness will fade. We're human. We have needs and desires, we're easily scared and easily amused. We're bright and intelligent. And most of all, we have an incredible capacity for learning and for change. We communicate with Gods and Demons, and Demons and Gods communicate with us.

There is madness all around, but we are the sane ones, and the madness will fade.

Next stop: reincarnation!

Most of us feel our existence makes sense if we are noticed by someone, preferably someone who loves us. So we try to make ourselves seen and heard. We try to show other people our lives, show them our emotions, convince them of our convictions. We twist and shout, we make a noise. And as we go about our days, all this adds up to something or someone, and that 'something or someone' is who we are.

It is important who we are. It matters how we act, and our words have meaning. It matters how we think, because how we think changes how we act. More than any of that, it matters how we understand the world around us and how we exude that understanding. Therefore, it is important how we define ourselves. What defines us as humans, is the way we use the wealth that comes with being alive in a living world. It is not how we want to be seen, it is not how we can make a show of ourselves, it is how we regard the animate and the inanimate, and how we show through our actions that we are aware of our own place in this adventure we call our life. It's our appreciation of happiness that shows the others who we are and what they mean to us.

In the world of the living beings, certainly in the human realm, the potential for happiness is limited by time and the way we treat each other. In the world of the Godhead though, everything is possible and there is an unbelievable abundance of the material and the immaterial. Abundance is the default state of the Life Force and there are no time restrictions. This also means the information given to the Godhead gets worked out far beyond any human limitation.

If you believe the world out there - that is: the lands, the clouds, the mountains, the seas - if you believe these are dead things, then it follows you, too, are merely something waiting to die. We know enough to realise that we have come from these dead things and we will return there. If you believe the world in essence is dead, then it's just that through some miracle you are alive now, but then death is your true state of being - and this is what you project.

A lot of people seem to think that indeed, the world is mostly dead, and they treat their fellow beings the way they see the world. They mow down the forests and they shoot elephants, they poison the earth, and they consume what they can consume and then spit out whatever they can't swallow. Animal life is worth nothing to them, monkeys are no safer than pigs. People whom they should consider their brothers and sisters are suffering, but they let them suffer. Because they ignore the lives of the people around them, they betray the world of the Gods, and in turn they are seen as nothing more than as bringers of death and betrayal.

It is a sad way of being, living a life as though somehow forced to be a solitary individual defined by death and betrayal. And what's more, there is an alternative to these beliefs. Why not believe the world is a living force and all that is out there is connected just so as to create life and to sustain life? Why not believe you are seen by the planet and the planet does not betray you? All you have to do is acknowledge that the plants and the animals are as much a part of this world as humans are. You are here now, and you will be here tomorrow. When your body is gone, the essence of you - that is: The Eternal Heart - goes on to live through the others.

We only have to acknowledge that all the living things, including us, come from the earth, we go to the earth, and we arise out of that earth again. All of us are the children of our children, we are all children of the earth, and therefore we have a responsibility towards the earth. When you do this, your life suddenly becomes filled with meaning. It doesn't matter that some things are alive now and won't be alive in the future, nor does it matter that one day your body will be gone too. What matters is that the living things are connected, and they flow from one state into another. The good things are in a constant state of flux and they are dedicated to the renewal of life. The life you feel inside every single day, is the same life that means the difference between a barren planet and a flowering earth.

This life is not ours. We didn't invent life, and we can't create it either. But we know what suffering means, and the thing is that if we continue to create societies as though death and suffering are what define us, then indeed, death and suffering will soon be the only things we'll see. Of these 'Death' is not the most interesting aspect of our being here, 'Life' is. Death is nothing to worry about, it will inevitably come. The thing is that while we're alive we'd all probably like to avoid suffering. And because we reincarnate in some shape or form, we cannot escape the suffering that we cause, not now nor in the future. So we'd be wise to spend our days engaged in finding a way of living that does not simultaneously hold the promise of a barren earth.

What defines us as human beings is not the fact that we struggle and worry, it is how we care about the Life Force living through us. Human interactions, the day to day routines and rituals, the buying and selling, the loving and longing - this can all be a way to express how we want to be connected to the living world, to each other and to the world of the Gods. We're here to stay in some shape or form, so why be defined by betrayal and death? Instead, we should all try to express ourselves through connection and through life. When we all define ourselves as messengers to the Gods, all our actions are messages. The messages we send are seen and heard, now and forever.

Love and Beauty

Love is invisible in everything, Beauty is visible everywhere. Love wants to connect and in that connection is Beauty. Love is a strength and not a weakness. She will connect to everything she may connect with. She shall connect to the precious and the good, and to sadness, to desire, to anger and to fear. Out of sorrow and anger worlds have been created, through desire mountains have been moved; and always there was Love and there was Beauty.

Love goes 'bump' in the night, and then may never show her face during the day. This love-thing is much sung about, yet, like the Eternal Heart, it is nothing to hold on to. Love moves inside of all animals, you can feel Her, but you can't ever touch. And that's not all. Love is a spirit, trying to move from the invisible world into the visible one. She is a Force that will live when all else is gone. Which is not to say it is benign. Trying to be expressed, Love creates alliances with other forces, and in the process may transform into something altogether more insidious. Sometimes it's hard to distinguish between

Love and Evil, as both can be in league with Anger.

Two stories come to mind. One is a newspaper clipping I read when I was in my late teens, concerning a woman who had murdered her husband. She had fallen in love with another man, and so her longtime husband had to go. For reasons that were rather mysterious to her once the act had been performed, she had seen no other way to regain the freedom she needed for being with her new lover than killing the old lover.

The other story dates back a little farther. One day three goddesses were waging a beauty contest. They asked a young man named Paris to judge. The goddess of Love, a certain Aphrodite, was not above a little bribery, and she promised Paris he could have the most beautiful woman on earth if he'd declare Aphrodite to be the prettiest. Paris was easily swayed, proclaimed Aphrodite the winner, and a short while later came to collect his prize. This most beautiful woman on earth was called Helena, and she was married to the king of Sparta. Marriage was not exactly something the Greek Gods cared much about, and so Aphrodite abducted Helena and delivered her to Paris' bed in the fair city of Troy. Next thing you know, it's war between the Greeks and the Trojans, and the earth is stained with the blood of the heroes. Drama abounds. Little known fact: After their victory, the Greek army burned down the city of Troy, reunited Helena with her king, and they lived happily ever after.

Both these stories are love stories, and they will quicken the pulse as well as rattle the mind. However, they will probably not warm the heart, unless you have a very specific type of heart, one that's into tales of the macabre.

At this point, I want to try to give some kind of definition of what I think 'Desire' and 'Longing' are. I think desire belongs to the visible world, and longing belongs to the world of the invisible. So 'desire' is something that can be known and described, more or less. I think all of us have some idea of what we desire, at least when we see it. Desires may not be very well-defined, but they can be put into words. For instance, you know when you desire a certain body or a certain status or even an entire life with its specific trimmings.

On the other hand, 'longing' is a far heavier brew. The liquid of longing is always simmering in a kettle filled with the pain of being born, with trauma, with memories of dreams and past lives, with sexual pleasure that is as sweet as it is bitter, and most of all this liquid of longing is brewed in the realm of Demons. The longing stems from a dark place where all that can be talked about in the world of desire is now beyond the reach of words. If anything, this love-longing can be referenced through sounds and images, and black magic.

I believe that when you're falling in love, what you think is that the person you're falling for somehow has the potential to fulfil your desires. Contrary to that, what you feel is a dark longing flowing through you. What you feel is a need that has its roots on the beach where mankind was born out of the spirit world. Maybe Love is the plant that grows from these roots, a plant that has been living in the mud and that has been fed on the longing. And on the branches of this love-plant grow flowers that give off a heavy perfume and that will give fruits that are the colour of blood.

When you say 'I love you', you refer to this love-plant growing in the mysterious greenhouse of your soul. The longing is trying to overtake you and envelop you and then swallow you whole. So when I'm talking about love, I also mean this kind of love, the kind of love that comes to you in a dream but is not exactly the stuff of romance. I'm talking about a greedy kind of love, an unholy alliance of lust and rage that will propel you forwards regardless of your best interests. It is clear that people want to be in league with the two-faced demon of Love, but it is also clear that we need to be aware of what we are dealing with.

This is where the notion of Beauty comes in. Beauty is a symbol representing 'desire'. What is really meant by 'Beauty' is, in fact, 'the desire to experience beauty'. Beauty connects to the material world, rather than just point towards a thing that is aesthetically pleasing in and of itself. Beauty makes itself known on the inside of a person, it is an indication of desires that might be fulfilled. This is why beauty is closely connected to the physical experience, it works its way outside in. Love endows what it desires with beauty. All that is loved is beautiful. In this way, it is through love and beauty that our lives are connected to the visible and the invisible worlds. That is why we should search for beauty in our lives, and direct our efforts towards creating beauty.

Beauty is what we should all be concerned with. Beauty and violence do not mingle. When there is beauty, it ought to be appreciated, not mistaken for the object of one's desires, certainly never taken with violent means. The beautiful experience is tied to the kind of love that reaches out to help and connect. This experience is something a society can help bring about, for its own sake and for the sake of its citizens. As a society, we may not be able to expect the others to be loving all the time, nor can we expect ourselves to have loving feelings without interruption, but we can always take care that our actions lead to the experience of beauty.

On a day-to-day level, seeing beauty equals a careful approach to whatever is out there. You want the experience to last, so you have to let go of desire, and breathe. An alliance with Love means opening your eyes, breathing in and out, and finding beauty. Then, once you found it, experience it, do not try to steal it away. Whatever it is that strikes you as beautiful, that is where you may direct your attention. Do you feel the good kind of Love inside, the kind that lifts you up, and that shows the face of beauty? Or is the Love Demon trying to break your heart?

Mag Ela

Maybe now is a good time to talk about me. Who is this man speaking to you? Is it a man at all? Where do these thoughts come from? Are they thoughts or merely quotations without quotation marks? Why does he - if it is a 'he' - want you to know all this?

Well. The writer identifies as male, this I will admit. He has a body that he considers to be of the male variety, and so far it has served him well. There is nothing to be inferred from this though, it is a mere statement of a perceived fact. Facts are not what make up a person's story, neither mine nor yours. They are just things that have come about or that currently are happening, what matters are the lessons received and the insights brought.

I have been called many things, some not so very flattering.

I have tried out various names. Names are just pointers, they only mean what you want them to mean, and mostly they don't mean anything. If your 'real' name is the name your parents gave to you at birth, why should this naming by people who hardly knew you be more real than a name you choose for yourself? I take on a new name whenever I feel it's appropriate, and I will revert to any old name whenever this is helpful. I will not allow for myself to be shackled by a name that I don't care for to a world that I have left behind.

I have tried out many professions. Sometimes I was met with financial success and the approval of my peers, other times nothing much came of it. It is all equal, if you ask me. Success feels different from failure, though, so I'd rather have success. But, to paraphrase Epicurus the prophet, it's better to fail at something worthwhile than to succeed at something that is ultimately worthless.

In matters of romance, I have often wondered who is this 'me'? As a lover and a friend, I have been a fool and an idiot, as ignorant as the next man. I have acted callous and careless. I am aware of that, and all I can hope for is that I have done little harm.

I found myself violently striving for something while wondering who it was that behaved in a fashion that I disapproved of.

What was going on in this mind that I call 'my mind', and why did I call it mine when there hardly seemed to be an 'I' controlling it? This duality of thought and action was a constant source of bewilderment. I succumbed to the lure of action without having any proper framework with which to judge my actions, let alone adjust them in a good way. Ageing changed things somewhat, but you can't cure all ills just with the passing of time.

However, I always had this notion of something living near to me, hiding in the shadows. The sensation of a hand touching me on occasions when I was all alone. A sense that a house I entered did not appear empty, even though it had been vacated long ago. A voice calling in the night, sounds that made no sense. The feeling of connecting to another person's soul rather than to their personality. This didn't add up to anything much though, it just had me wondering.

Then the car crash happened, along came this destructive love, the world changed, and nothing seemed to make much sense anymore. And then it did. Now I know there is not just a tunnel, there is also a light. There are many people out there lost in this foggy netherworld, trying to see what lies beyond this world of ego and unconscious action. Maybe that is you, reading this book, because you noticed there is something here that is calling out to you.

The Faith that I'm trying to impart on you has come to me via many ways. Watching movies with impenetrable plot lines, or, with inane cliches, showed me the notion of a 'greater consciousness' that was showing itself. Trying to find a space that was empty, that was not 'me' nor 'Self', helped. Talking to friends who had gone through similar experiences or had had completely different experiences showed me another kind of life that could have been mine, too. Texts that I have once read and that never made sense to me, suddenly started to make sense as I began to realise that these texts were a continuation of earlier tales, and these tales all referenced the undercurrent of the world. I have found this Faith, because my mistakes have showed me other choices could have been made as well, it is just that at the time I was too concerned with wrestling demons that I didn't even realise existed. Becoming aware that I am this thing that is just passing on is helpful.

I've been a fool and an idiot way too often. I have put my trust in a belief that tricks us all into thinking wealth equals luxury. But I'm beginning to see the light. In fact, I am finally beginning to see the beauty of this world, and I want you to also see this beauty.

The Snake of Chaos rears its ugly head again

Beauty and chaos are odd bed-fellows. So, let's again take a close look at this demonic reptile.

The Snake of Chaos is a well-know beast of myth. Every now and again it rears its head and wags its tail. Sometimes it looks like a dragon, and a knight comes to slay it. At other times, it hangs out in orchards and seduces young women into taking a bite out of an apple. In the myths of ancient Egypt, it takes on its most interesting form. There, the Snake of Chaos came into being at the beginning of the world, and it never went away. It lives in the Underworld amidst the lost souls. At night the Gods Horus and Seth unite with the Pharaoh to travel the Underworld and battle the beast. During the day, these Gods are not so very united, and they try to gain power over the world of the living. As the Gods quarrel, the leaders of men maintain order the best way they see fit.

Somehow it seems that people are always the dupe. Either they have to await the coming of a saviour, i.e. Saint George to come and slay a bit, or they are thrown out of the garden where life is good, and sent off to live in a world of toil and trouble. For the Egyptians of antiquity too, during the day they were subjected to the whims of the Gods in cahoots with the Pharaoh, while at night they were left on their own as a battle was raging supposedly in their best interests. In brief, the people never had much say in their own struggle with chaos.

In the early years of Christianity, things were not so clear-cut. There were many cults and different ways to worship. After all, the Romans were the rulers of the world, and they had a veritable panoply of Gods. Not just the well-known ones like Jupiter and Bacchus, there were Gods for every household as well. The Roman pantheon was in many ways a continuation of the Greek divine universe, but the Romans incorporated Gods from the occupied territories too, and put them alongside the Roman Gods. For instance, the Egyptian God Isis had it its own temple in Rome, where Roman dignitaries came to worship under the guidance of Egyptian priests. The people were there for the Gods, and the Gods were there for the people.

In this world of Gods, the Christians were an anomaly with their view of a single God, not quite the YHWH of the Jews, who created everything and ruled supreme. At the time though, the Christian world was divided among itself. A strong counter-current existed to what we now think of as 'Christianity'. Although inspired by Jesus, other groups held a contrary view of what Jesus' story implied for the image of God-the-Creator. The best-known of these contrary believers were the 'Gnostics', and they were not regarded well by the Christians that would eventually create the ruling church.

In Gnostic thought, the snake that seduced Eve is not such a bad creature at all, instead the problem originates at the Creator-God. Adam and Eve are kept in the dark as to their true nature, and it is the snake that offers them salvation by suggesting they eat the apple of the Tree of Wisdom. Once they've taken a bite, they see that they are Gods themselves, and it is at that moment that they realise that they are 'created in the image of God', meaning that they are equal to Him. In this vision, the Creator-God is not the good guy, because he subsequently casts people into his world of matter, where their Divine spirit is locked inside the physical body. In the material world, they now have to struggle to get by. Thus, the Snake of Chaos is the bringer of wisdom, and it is only by accepting Chaos and rejecting the lure of the material world that we, people, can connect to our divine origin. According to the Gnostics, Jesus has shown the way out of the fixed, material world, and into a world where the spirit is once more free to roam.

Interestingly, in some Gnostic texts there appears the notion of a greater God. This 'greater God' is the blueprint for the divine nature of people, the very divinity that has been taken from them by the God who created the Material World. This greater God is an abstract being along the lines of Brahma, but it is also sometimes seen as a female figure, as 'God the Mother' or the 'Mater Magna', the 'Great Mother'. There even exist gnostic texts in which the Creator-God is berated for claiming He has created everything. And, on a side note, in the Old Testament this God the Creator seems well aware that He's not the only God out there. After all, why demand that the people worship only Him if there are no other Gods that could also be worshipped?

I suggest we create the Snake of Chaos in our own image. Let's think of the Snake of Chaos not as our enemy, but, instead, as a metaphorical way of talking about human nature and the nature of the world surrounding us. Chaos means freedom. And so, as things stand, we now have to find a balance between an overwhelming world of unlimited potential and a world in which we need to connect to Love and Beauty as well as take care of the short-term survival of the body. So much to do, so little time to do it in. Chaos also implies choice.

Coming back to the world of the Gods. What would be really helpful is to have another story that sheds some light on how we got to be in this world that is halfway between the gutter and the stars. A world in which we are surrounded by Gods and Demons sailing the dark seas of senseless being, while we are living in these bodies, caught in a society - or let's say, caught in an ideology - that seems to be on a collision course with the very planet that sustains us.

The Good Life is what we're after, so we need to find a way to learn to live with chaotic and destructive impulses, and then, instead, use these impulses as building blocks for a road to happiness. How can the Gods show us a way to the balanced life we need, if Epicurus didn't do so already? The story that we can use in order to talk about our lives is a story of the war of the Gods, with people getting caught in the middle.

The war of the Gods

The Eternal Unity came to the earth in the shape of a bird, with wings like clouds. Between her claws she carried a seed made from air and fire. She wrapped it in a blanket made from the knowledge of good and wonder, so that the seed would not be damaged. She floated above the earth looking for a place to land, but she did not find any, until she came to the island of Arcadia. There, she halted and she buried the seed in the fertile soil. A plant rose from it, and from this plant fell two people like fruits to the earth. The Eternal led them to a river, from which two spirits rose up, the beautiful Niobe and the handsome Nerites. Together they had many daughters and many sons. These people were kind and good, and The Eternal gave them over into the hand of Eleima, the Earth Goddess, after which She returned to the stars and became a blinding sun.

The first people lived in the vicinity of the Earth Goddess, careless, without anger or sorrow. They were at peace with one another and shared what came to them in a community of equals. The stiffness of old age did not come to them, their limbs stayed as supple as at birth. Every night they lay at great banquets, without any evil thoughts, because all the good things were there for the gathering: On the fields, plants grew in abundance, and the trees carried ample fruits. When the time would come to leave the body behind, these people were led to a peaceful place by the daughters of Eleima, where they went as if in sleep. In this life and in this death, they were like the equals of Eleima, they were like the gentle ghosts watching over the people and keeping them from injustice and loneliness.

Kelaino, the envious Moon God, watched the joy of his sister, and how the people lived under her guidance. He shone his light on the path the people had to go, but he forgot the words of The Eternal when She gave the earth to Eleima and the moon to him. His light faltered during the day and at night it sometimes shone bright and sometimes dim.

Kelaino came to the world and begat himself sons. The sons swarmed out unto the people and whispered in their ears to go search for silver and gold. They promised the people that the magnificent lustre of these metals would bring great happiness, and Kelaino shone the light of the moon to reveal the gold they desired. Those who figured themselves king, he warned against other kings elsewhere, living in palaces bigger and more impressive. To the people who were happy tilling the land, people who asked no more than they needed, the sons said: You are a king, the holy flame burns within you as brightly as it burns within kings. Why do you have to work here, why would you take from the land no more than you need? You may sell the surplus, you can be rich, you may clothe yourself in the softest dresses. What use living with the animals as though they are your equals and their blood is as valuable as yours? Take from everything there is as much as you can take and then take more. This earth has been given to the people, take all it has to offer. Time is going by, soon you will be old and weak, who will protect you? Who will come to save you if you have no gold to offer?

This way, they poisoned their minds, and hence from the people came new-borns that did not resemble the first happy race in any way. The second race was suspicious and hungry, nor in body nor in mind like the first had been. Sons stayed under the care of their mothers until many years had passed, they were involved in simple sports and games, like children. And when these boys finally became adults in the strength of their years, they didn't last long and their days were filled with useless lust and superfluous works. Their main goal was attaining greater power over one another. No longer did they honour the Goddess, not in thought and not through the partaking in sacrificial rites. When they finally shed their mortal shape, they went without dignity, like beasts in great panic.

The daughters of Eleima saw the many temptations with which Kelaino and his sons infuriated the people, they saw the fear the sons put into the hearts of this second race, and the daughters felt a heavy burden upon them. All too readily the people were led astray. And it couldn't be denied that there was great beauty in the world. Beautiful hides came from wild animals, from the thick wool of sheep, colourful blankets were weaved, the oldest trees served to build the hardiest houses. In light of the bounty of the earth, it seemed ungrateful not to partake in all this. And if the people went through great travails to dig out treasures from the deep, who could deny them their pride at receiving such rewards in exchange for their aspirations? Who could fault them for not wanting to leave behind what they had gathered with their own blood, even if it wasn't of any use to them?

The voices of the daughters sounded ever more faint, no longer could they lead people unto any road at all. The daughters turned to their mother and asked her counsel: O great Mother! You who has spread the gifts of The Eternal on earth, who guarded over the first people when they were born out of the love of The Unity, tell us how to help the people now. We wish to do your work and show them the joy of The Returning, but our voices go unheard.

At that time on the island Mycene lived a man of whom it was told he was like the blacksmith of the Gods. The Goddess turned to him, she gave him a stone loaded with iron, and said: My daughters need your help. From this rock, build them a servant who is stronger than the sons may ever be, one whose voice never gets lost and whose light glows from the inside.

The blacksmith, who according to his nature wanted to do whatever he was asked, took to work. He lowered the iron into his most blazing oven and for three days and three nights he hit the rock with his mighty hammers. As the blows hit the rock, the iron ore threw off the darkness of the earth and a great light started to shine. The more the iron glowed, the faster the blacksmith made his hammers land. In the heat of the forge they seemed one like water and fire at the time when the Earth was still young.

On the fourth day he opened his oven and showed Eleima the results of his work. There, amidst marble shapes, a small boy lay asleep. All around him a light shone as if The Unity had been reborn, and in his chest a perfect heart beat pace. Eleima called him Eleutherios, the liberator. She thanked the smith and took the child in her arms. She left the smithy and went outside, where summer had come. In the light of the sun she studied the fine traits of the child's face, she heard its tender sighs and she looked at its fine fingers. How will this child ever be able to help my daughters? She wondered, but instantly she felt a great love for him and she trusted the blacksmith' knowledge.

She gave the boy over to her daughters Adrasteia en Ide to watch over him and then sent them on their way.

When Kelaino heard Eleima had turned to the blacksmith for help, he feared his sister had come up with a ruse. Disguised as a young man, he also turned to the smith, and he said: I am the son of a shepherd, but no longer are my services needed. My father has sent me out into the world to learn what it is my family needs to do to be able to survive. I beg you to show me the secrets of the fire, so I may serve the people and may keep my sisters from hunger.

The good blacksmith took the boy under his guidance and showed him the skills for many years. Kelaino learned how the iron may be broken from the earth, how separate metals may become as one. He was taught the art of turning raw materials into pleasing implements, how to turn useless gold into new suns, and to sculpt the most inspiring ornaments from the largest rocks. And after he had learned all this, Kelaino thanked the smith for his goodwill, and finally he made himself a new hammer, stronger than any known before.

But Kelaino didn't use his knowledge to do good. He returned to the island Hades, and built a new smithy, and in the middle of his workplace he split the earth open with his hammer. He had his sons bring the people who couldn't die; and they also brought him people who died with so much fury that they were at once born again. These people he sent into the deep and he made them look for dark stones. From these stones he made hammers for his sons and he told them: Take your tool and travel to the far corners of the world. There you shall make your own smithy and from the fire and the earth you will make me so many new people that the daughters of Eleima will be no more than mere bystanders.

The sons went forth, only two stayed with Kelaino to serve him and keep those that were neither living nor dead locked up in the earth. Then one day these toiling people brought forth from the dark a rock of gold so immense it blocked the way to Kelaino's smithy. Because of this, the people stayed locked behind in the dark, where Kelaino and his sons could no longer control them. These people fled farther into the gloom and they sought their refuge there.

With his mighty hammer Kelaino hit the rock, but it withstood his violence for a long time. Whereupon he made a gigantic fire all around it, setting fire to all the smithy, and he hammered the gold ore with all his might. Finally he became exhausted, being naked under the sun. To cool down he swept big waves from the ocean and extinguished the blaze. The water and the fire made a bellowing cloud of steam, so nothing was visible anymore. But when a cool breeze blew the clouds away, in front of Kelaino's eyes a most magnificent creature rose from the earth. She had the face of a shy young girl and wore a sparkling dress with a golden girdle. Around her shoulders she wore a richly decorated scarf, a treasure in itself, with flowers that had been woven artfully through the texture. On her head she wore a golden wreath, as bright as any sun, on which all kinds of animals were portrayed as if alive.

Kelaino saw her there, having come from the deep earth, forged from fire and washed with water, she herself as pure as the air. She was the most magnificent being he had ever laid eyes upon, and he realised that the son of Eleima, the one moulded from hardened iron by the blacksmith, could be overcome by this creature who was in every way his equal. Not just in beauty, in kindness too, this creature equalled the son of Eleima: In the heat of the weld all the darkness from the underworld had fallen from her, and Kelaino feared that she might only bring happiness to Eleima's son. At this, he swept all the dust of his workplace together and put it in a wooden box. Brought together, the dust became a foul and poisonous mixture in which all manner of diseases and plagues fed upon each other with shameless cruelty, bitter greed and cowardly treason.

Kelaino named the girl Charis, the artful, and he said to her: I hereby name you the guardian of this box, which you may never open. Find the son of Eleima and make this a present to him, and when he has opened this box he will know what to do. After he has accepted your gift, quickly return to me, so that I may have the pleasure of your company once more. He gave her his two sons to carry the box and send her on her way.

Meanwhile the other sons of Kelaino had gone out into the world, into the most faraway places. They made their workplaces everywhere, as their father had ordered them. But the knowledge of Kelaino was imperfect and he had only passed imperfect knowledge on to his sons. In their smithies the sons made many mistakes, and they didn't pay proper attention to the kind of people they planted on the world in high numbers.

The people that had been created thus did not resemble the first and not even the second race. They were a terrible breed, half man, half animal, satisfied only with destructive works and waging war with each other. Their hearts were made from molten stone and the little tenderness they knew was locked away in the cage of their enormous bodies. They were as strong as giants, with long arms, with great coarse hands, and in every manner they resembled the recklessness of the sons who had no idea what they had created. And when these giants finally died because of each other's violence, the sons took them to their smithies and had them work the dark underground.

As the people of Kelaino's sons roamed the earth, the son of Eleima grew up in the prosperous land of Nysa, in a place hidden between mountains and valleys. He had become a beautiful young man, with soft traits and legs like a deer. In the company of the two daughters that Eleima had asked to guard over him, he practised the arts, and together they sang many songs as they travelled through the woods and learned from all that lived there.

Rivers of milk and rivers of wine flowed over the land of Nysa, and rivers of nectar of bees. The Liberator went forth until he came to a place where the tired Charis was sat on the moss next to the box of Kelaino. The two sons were leaning against it. Charis opened her eyes and saw the beautiful boy before her, and she knew he meant her no harm.

He gave her water to drink, and she said: I have come on behalf of my father, who offers you this chest. I am told it contains a great treasure which I must guard until it is in your hands. But although I must honour my father, his task has brought me nothing but suffering. We wandered through endless forests where no animals dared walk, and we wandered through barren fields where nothing would grow. His task has made us taste nothing but hunger. Deliver me from this bitter gift, so I and my servants may go in freedom.

Eleima's son heard her voice. He saw the depth of her eyes, and he wished to relieve her of her burden. He took her hand, and said to her: I shall take this gift from you, so that you are released of your burden, yet I shall not accept it. Only that which you desire to give is of value to me, because my reward is to accept your joy, and I derive no joy from that which you were merely ordered to give. A father who makes his daughter suffer will not be honoured by me.

He asked the sons to take the chest to a nearby cave and leave it there. He himself picked the fruit off a tree and offered it to the girl so she could satisfy her hunger. Relieved of her hunger, she feasted, then joyfully lay herself down next to him. When Charis was sleeping, the Liberator made for the woods.

After the sons of Kelaino had left the chest behind, they went on their separate ways. When one of them saw a deer, he did not hesitate for a moment and shot at it with his arrows. He then chipped the body into seven pieces and cooked them, and roasted them over a fire. He tossed the entrails aside, and he did not notice that the heart was still beating. Meanwhile, the other son had found some fruit and returned to his brother. He saw him by the fire with his victim, and cried out: You wretch! What have you done? What were you thinking, to kill a child and eat it? If we were not doomed before, then now we are so! Stop this disgusting meal immediately, burn your food down to the last morsel, sacrifice everything you have, and beg for the Gods to be merciful. And he took the heart, hid it in a cloth, and ran away from his brother.

So Charis found him again. She had been looking for the brothers while she was still deep in thought of the Liberator. She was told of the great misfortune. The girl was taken entirely unawares. Her head became like water, the strength left her legs and she collapsed into his arms. The good son lifted her up and so they left these beautiful shores in despair.

The other son was equally dispirited, but his fear and fright had made him forgetful of his brother's instructions. Instead of building an altar for his sacrifice, he made himself a fire as of a forge. He had also been given a hammer by his father, and he thought to make a new boy from the bones. He took three bronze coins, placed the bones on them and heated a fire around it. His fire had not yet caught, and his hammer had yet to deliver its first strikes, but the earth burst open and melted entirely. The coins melted like ice on a sunny day, they became like boiling oil, the rocks melted and the liquid rocks splashed off the ground high up in the air, as though the entire earth was a pot boiling on a blazing fire. In the places where the incandescent pieces fell, the earth tore open again, and from the tears there flowed blood that touched the flames, only to become another blazing fire.

The disaster spread further and further. The workshops of Kelaino's other sons were also reached, and they went up in a roar of flames. The forests and the woods, the fields full of grain, even the seas were poisoned, and there was nowhere left to hide. In all places reached by the flames, the people perished, and the sons of Kelaino and the daughters of Eleima perished with them, and their spirits drifted in the air like wisps of smoke.

From his workplace, Kelaino saw how the fire devoured the good and the bad around it without discerning. The chest that he had made for Eleima's son was also touched by the flames, so that it burst open and the filth spread like a cloud over the land that had hitherto been untouched. The last people who remained there were hit by this choleric gift and blinded by fear and insanity, they now turned on one another. The earth would soon be like the moon, only more tarnished, with her green fields extinguished.

Only Adrasteia and Ide, the daughters of Eleima that she had sent with her son were still safe. They now cared for the son of Kelaino and over Charis with the Heart. The Goddess led them to an untouched well where many animals had also fled to. And while the earth was burning, they all hid far under the surface of the water.

New explosions followed. The seas evaporated. Volcanos raised their lava until finally the well with the Liberator in it was also covered in a layer of rocks, and everything that was in the well now sunk into the earth. Yet this did not bring joy to Kelaino. He no longer relished the jealousy that had driven him. Bitter tears welled up in his eyes and he fell to his knees and roared.

Finally, the fire was extinguished and the earth was ashen and inhospitable. After centuries, Kelaino lifted his head and he saw his sister standing beside him. The children of the Mother-Father were now equals. They were discharged from their duties. They could no longer serve The Unity.

Eleima spoke to her brother: You have shown the people your powers and where are they now? You have robbed me of my treasures and what has it brought you? You have turned your children against mine and what has become of them? We were together as Desire and Beauty, and now we are neither of those, and then what are we?

And Kelaino answered: Your beauty was too much for me, I could not possess it and have stolen it from you. I know what has brought me to do so, and I seek no forgiveness. There is no forgiveness for those who know what is right, yet do what is wrong. I shall leave your earth and wait in the dust between the stars for the Eternal to take me to Her in Her mercy.

But Eleima said: Forget the insanity of the world that has been, and let us form a new covenant. I have hidden within this earth that which shall always be good. I hid my son and your daughter in the only clear well. Next to them I put the most beautiful part of you and the best part of me.

Eleima took Kelaino's hammer and beat the rocks aside, so that the water in which she had kept the peace became visible. In this water a mighty tree grew from the heart of the Liberator. Its roots dug deeply into the earth and its leaves reached high into the sky. On this tree grew apples and plums, pears and oranges and all other kinds of fruit. Vines wrapped around the trunk and offered great bunches of grapes. Birds and all kind of animals fell from these vines, and they feasted on little plants that sprouted from the roots of the tree, growing all kinds of berries amidst the most beautiful flowers.

Eleima broke two branches from the tree and dipped them into the water. She stuck the one branch into the earth by the leaves, and the fruits of the field grew from there. She took the other branch to the country of Eleusia, where she buried it in the earth, and this branch sprouted mysterious fruits in strange shapes. The fruits tasted bitter and showed great secrets to all who ate them, but it is said they were guarded by the Great Snake of Chaos.

Under the tree of the Liberator sat the children of Charis and Kelaino's son, the fourth and last people. They mixed into many shapes, freed of their heavy burden; from them came women and men and all the beings that are man nor woman. The divine was visible in them as it was destined to be. But Kelaino said: It is a hopeless life on this earth if there is no return to The Unity. That way, every day is the same day, only worse, beauty offers merely insanity, and food offers only the expectation of hunger or excess. That way, the young do not display their powers, and they will perish like the old, only more slowly. War lurks in all reason and the seeds of new battle are present in all peaceful moments.

And Eleima answered: People are like leaves that long to return to the tree. The desire is their fate, but the return is their destiny. Time on earth is intended for them to do what they deem right. Evil can be done, although they will not benefit from it. You and I have this covenant now, and we shall keep the people so that they may be messengers to us.

The falling leaves

So there you have it. This earth we live on is the result of the God of the Material World doing battle with the Goddess of the Invisible World. Their antagonism and envy have led to fear and chaos, to destruction, and finally, to present-day humanity. Wo/mankind is like a fallen leaf that longs to return to its tree. Poetics aside, what are we talking about?

This story could just be another variation on the age-old 'warring gods create the world' theme. There is a twist though. When she finds herself battling her envious brother, Eleima, the Goddess of the invisible world, turns to the blacksmith who creates her a son. This son is called 'Eleutherios', which means 'The Liberator'. The God of the material world, Kelaino, subsequently steals the knowledge of the blacksmith, and creates himself a daughter to defeat Eleima's son. His creation is called Charis, 'the artful one', which might be interpreted as an indication for the deceit or trickery she is meant to use against Eleutherios. So it's an arms race, and as these things go, it turns out badly. Also, because it is a myth, out of the ashes a new world arises, and the mythological cycle of creation and destruction begins anew.

It seems Kelaino wins. Charis really does cause the downfall of Eleutherios, and her poisonous gift really is brought into this world. It's not her fault, but nonetheless, the damage is done. Deceit trumps Liberty, and it is only thanks to the wisdom of the Goddess Eleima that in the end something good comes out of the whole mess and life is regenerated. However, if that was all there is to it, that would not be a hopeful story. Inconsistent, too. Why is the son of the Goddess called The Liberator, when he has merely served as food for the dumbest of Kelaino's sons? Why is Charis 'the artful one' when she seems to do no more than stumble from mishap into misery?

This is what I think the story means. Both Charis and Eleutherios have come into the world as tools of the Gods. Eleima has created her son Eleutherios to bring about peace, so that is his purpose. When Kelaino sends Charis off to carry a box to him filled with all things bad, unbeknownst to Kelaino, Eleutherios also carries a gift, a Heart. Not just an ordinary heart, this one keeps beating after the body has gone. So, this is 'the Eternal Heart'. As noted before, the Eternal Heart is the 'Self beyond the Self'. The Heart is the connection between the materialisation and the immaterial being of the Divine. So, from the beginning, Eleutherios has carried with him this Divine connection, and he was destined to show a troubled world the way out of the war. When Eleutherios forsakes his attachment to the material world, he doesn't die, quite the contrary, he returns to his purest form.

Charis' task mirrors the task of Eleima's son. Far from being a witless accomplice to her father's evil plans, Charis really is artful. Her name doesn't merely stand for trickery, it also stands for intelligence and inventiveness. In spite of the intentions of her father, she is the guardian of the Heart. Charis doesn't go back to the dark God, she takes care of the Heart of the Liberator. And when all seems lost, it is because of her that from this Heart the Goddess can create a new Tree of Life. The Liberator is the connection between the troubled world as-it-stands, and the promise of a better future.

Also, Eleima is charged with guiding the people through this world. When all seems lost, she has saved life in the waters, rescuing her daughters and Kelaino's son. Out of the children of the sons and daughters of the Gods come the new people. This myth shows that we are not the first, we are the fourth race instead, and we have come from many places. The Gods needed to learn, and to find their own peace first. Once the Gods were at peace, on the barren earth a new tree of life sprang from the heart of the Liberator. What's more, in the land of Eleusia, the Goddess has planted a branch from which a new Tree of Wisdom grows fruits that reveal great mysteries. That tree is guarded by the Snake of Chaos, because wisdom comes at a price. Wisdom may come when hardships have been suffered, and when dangers have been overcome.

Eleutherios is The Liberator, because, to this day, he shows how we, children of the children of the Gods, can free ourselves. He symbolically shows how to leave attachment, anger, resentment and the other all-too human traits behind - in brief: how to stop fighting - and lead a peaceful life again. When the war has been brought to an end, the Liberator offers the Eternal Heart, so that the connection with The Unity is not severed. He leads the way back to the abundance that is to be found in nature. Thanks to the covenant of both Gods and thanks to the sacrifice of Eleutherios, people are now living in the world of the two Gods that have come out of the First One. We can find our own place by following the example of the Liberator. We need to leave our division behind, so that we can partake in the gifts of this new Tree of Life, and of the mysterious fruits that grow on the Tree of Wisdom under the tutelage of the Snake of Chaos.

The story ends with a conversation between the Gods that is directly aimed at us, the people living now. People are like leaves, Eleima says, that long to return to the tree.

Like leaves, people are attached to their attachment, but all attachment is futile. As people fall into the world, their thoughts go out to what they have left behind. What has been left behind, of course, is the hazy memory of a world where life is unproblematic and good. Now somehow they've fallen, and life seems to consist of longing and the unhappy knowledge that something has been lost. And this endless falling is what daily life is like for most. They fear the meeting with the ground. They fear what will come after.

Without direction, life on earth is a hopeless undertaking. Every day is the same day, only worse. For those who can't decide what is truly desirable, there is only the expectation of a long life and a senseless death. Without a greater belief, all beauty shows decay, food announces the expectation of hunger, the youngest don't show any strength and wither away like their elders. We need direction, or we will crumble like leaves in autumn.

If people are the leaves, then the tree is a symbol for the Godhead we call The Unity. The Unity is the perfect beginning and the perfect ending. The tree is the origin and the return, the coming into being and the return to abstract consciousness. The Unity is our common ancestry, as well as our common goal. The Unity is never absent: The Unity is always there, we are not separated, and we shall return to Her. If The Unity is represented as a tree, she is the Tree of Life, foreshadowing the tree that will grow out of the Heart of The Liberator.

People are like falling leaves, and we can't choose our fall. However, we can choose the way in which we float through the air. The time of our flight is ours, and we may do whatever pleases us. It's even possible to do evil, although no one will benefit by that. When we choose evil, the anger of our peers will meet us and we shall be buried under their anger. To do evil is a choice, but, clearly, we have other choices as well. Our best option is to think of our fall as the return to the light, and then we float through our lives as we gently return to a perfect harmony with the Eternal Mind.

Where we come from, is where we are going. This world has come from The Unity, and it will return to Her. The Supreme Mind is our origin and our destination. That is not of our own volition, there is nothing we can do or say to make it any different. Each person is a leaf on the tree of The Unity and each person will one day let go of that mighty tree, because that is the only way we can ever return to it.

Every living being is a fragment of The Unity, each person carries the seed of the divine within. The Liberator has shown how to plant this seed, and how to cultivate our original connection. Being people, we tend to get overwhelmed by nostalgia for a life we've never lived, and we forget how we are alive now, we forget we are floating through this world, and we forget that we have a future that need not be worrisome. We forget that while we are alive, the beauty of our flight through this life is what needs our attention. On this flight, we are guided by the Goddess Eleima, and so, the Faith that you are offered is the Faith of Eleima.

Without the direction of the Goddess, life on earth is a hopeless undertaking. Every day is the same day, only worse. This is why it's better to feel that we do have a direction: We come from The Unity and we will return to Her. And if we live according to the direction that has been shown by The Liberator, our fall through this world can be the most joyful thing we will ever experience.

A Contract of Social Joy

For now, we are alive in this world, and it's joy we want to further. The Liberator has shown a symbolic way, it is up to people to find their own, practical way. Sad to say, the history of what we refer to as 'civilisation' has more than its fair share of well-documented, inventive abuse, more than it has a history of the spreading of joy. Not to be preachy - good heavens, no! - but this kind of history is not really a laughing matter. As the story of the Gods has shown in the preceding chapters, when the rule of one over the other is established through violence, trickery and deceit, then the end result will be death and decay. I'm guessing probably most of us would like to postpone these for a while, at least in our own daily lives. Therefore, let's examine the idea of civilisation from a slightly different angle. Let's see how the example of The Liberator can help to change society into the joyful kind we need.

As noted, individualism is only conducive to joy when it is embedded in the bosom of a community. The reverse, a situation in which everyone feels like a solitary individual, leads to many having the sensation of being alone out in a dangerous world. In this state of loneliness, even in a crowd, there is a limited capacity for joy. On the downside, left alone, the individual is bereft of the advantages that come with living as part of a group of likeminded people. The notion of 'energy' that a community brings is missing, as is the comfort of safety in numbers, lesser individual effort, and the stability is absent that comes with being able to rely on one's support group of family and friends, or even on the greater support of 'the State'. On the upside, being a solitary individual also means one is free to do whatever the hell one pleases. Individualism allows for choosing to connect to whomever or whatever one wishes, without interference from a meddling society. Living alone may not be not entirely pleasant, yet it's not entirely unpleasant either. The solitary wo/man can choose their own destiny.

However, even when we may feel like we're basically alone, if everyone is just a leaf falling from the tree of the Godhead unto the soil that feeds the tree, we are all connected through our common destiny. It is in everybody's best interests to keep the tree alive and well. This implies some kind of organisation that strikes a balance between the interests of society and those of the individual. This is where a return to the philosophy of Jean-Jacques Rousseau (1712 - 1768) can help. He has already thought of ways to structure a new, more joyful society.

In his 1762 book 'Du contrat social, ou Principes du droit politique', Rousseau set out the theory of a 'social contract' between the state - acting through its government - and the citizens of that state. To sum up, Rousseau argued that people's interactions with the state at the time led to a situation worse than the one they were at even when living in isolation out in the wild. The state being able to muster force did not lend it legitimacy. Without legitimacy, there should be no rightful duty for anyone to submit to the state. In the 'social contract' he proposed, everyone forfeits the same number of rights and the same duties are imposed on all. The citizenry has a right to choose the laws under which they live, and the entire population, acting through the state, upholds their own laws. When the state government exceeds the boundaries agreed upon by the people, this government may be abolished and replaced.

Taking Rousseau's Social Contract as a starting point, I believe we need to think about a contract between community and individuals that incorporates the notion of Joy. I'm not talking about society providing entertainment and spectacle here, I'm not talking of reality t.v. and the pursuit of all things plastic, I'm talking about a deep, innate sense of life being good, and one's falling through time feeling like the flight one was meant to take. Every individual is a falling leaf, and it is the pleasurable task of the community to enable a joyful flight and to ensure a soft landing. The community, being made up of all individuals, in turn reaps the pleasure of knowing all will feel this joy in exactly the way that suits them best as individuals.

From this, it inevitably follows that individual pleasure is a matter for the community and communal pleasure is a matter for the individual. This does not imply that at any given moment, just to please them, anyone ought to give in to the whims and wishes of anyone else or even of the group, quite the contrary. The Social Contract of Joy sets a standard for behaviour of the group towards the Individual as well as for behaviour of the individual towards any other individual. Because everyone looks out for the joy of all the others, any act that is the result of coercion or pressure ought to be avoided. And because we don't always know what the others want or need, there will be free and open communication that is conducive to bringing about joy. When thinking of the biblical question, 'Am I my brother's keeper?', both as individuals and as a community, we should answer, 'Yes, I am. And I will show this by acting in a way that gives joy to them.'

The Social Contract of Joy is therefore in itself a thought-experiment intended to imagine what it means to think of our societies not just as human constructs, but also as the result of influences of unknown and unknowable Gods and Demons. Because these Gods and their ilk have their own interests, people are free to pursue human happiness in our world, although we would be unwise to forget about the world of the Gods. It's just that in that human pursuit there is always the notion of Joy being the foremost thing of worth, because through joy the Gods are informed upon the notion of happiness, while Demons are kept at bay.

Privacy, property, responsibility

Any kind of obligation of the individual towards the greater community implies a limitation of individual freedom. This makes for a moment's pause. History is rife with stories of individuals getting crushed in the name of a greater good or ideal that the community imposes upon them. Somehow, the ideals of the 'greater community' all too often seem to go in a direction that will not allow any of its citizens to unabashedly choose a course that will free them from the boundaries of society. Even when the greater community is mostly benign, there is a fine line between the state lending a helping hand and the state mostly enforcing the interests of the powerful members that dictate the rules that govern the community. On the other hand, it's not so easy to be out on your own, living a solitary life.

If the interests of the community take precedence over the interests of the individual, then private life is under attack. You can see this everywhere you look, because in almost any state, whether they are known as democracies or dictatorships, there are always reasons to rule every aspect of the life of individuals. It the Contract of Social Joy, such as I envisage, the notion of a private life is not abolished, but, instead, it is redefined. A private life, as expressed through intimate acts, is not to be offered up on the altar of the greater good, it is to be cherished. Intimacy is what most people long for, and so, society holds an interest in enabling a sphere where a private life, and intimate pleasures, can flourish. In the new world, this sphere is extended so that greater freedom is achieved.

For instance, many people find joy in religious or sexual activity. However, in most societies the expression of these acts is relegated to a private sphere where it is nonetheless subjected to community rule. This means that people are not completely free to have the kind of interactions that they desire, where they desire them, and with whomever they desire to have these interactions. They cannot have them in public, and they are not truly free to have them in private either. People are not free to have sex out in the streets, nor to go out and wear any kind of headgear they choose to represent their beliefs. Whenever they try, society quickly intervenes, which these days also means all of us are more or less constantly under electronic surveillance. This is problematic, because it limits the individual potential, which in turn generates a realm of fantasy that can easily lead to frustration and undesired violence. Sad to say, we are all fully aware of the way this has worked out in the past, and how it is working out every day still.

Therefore, when there is a society that has the best experience for all of its members at heart, an obviously joyful activity is not a private matter nor is it a communal matter. Things that bring joy and cause no harm are beyond the realm of judgement. Activities that bring joy should be deemed neutral. These activities, be they sexual or religious or what-have-you, are no matter for anyone who is not freely participating. The limitations imposed, if any, are merely there to ensure that this neutral zone is safe-guarded for the sake of the well-being of those who wish to indulge. This goes for any kind of activity that may be joyful if performed with the full and voluntary cooperation of all parties. For instance, not everyone wants to have sex with everyone else, there will always need to be a mutual desire, so it is the task of the community to ensure that there are sufficient means for all of its individual members to be open about their desires, as well as having their wishes respected. If an act that ought to be joyful has become depressing through the use of force, then the neutrality of the zone has been transgressed upon.

Whenever a transgression occurs, it is a matter for the community to act in such a manner that the possibility of joy is restored. Instead of a small group measuring out punishment to the transgressor, the entire community accepts its responsibility for the act of transgression, as well as for the act of reparation. After all, it is not just that an individual has disturbed the neutrality of the community, also the community finds its neutrality imposed upon. Because all individuals are members of the community, therefore all are imposed upon, and all are charged with the repair, which includes transgressor and transgressee.

This position is contrary to that of philosophers such as Garret Hardin (1915 - 2003), or his distant precursor Thomas Hobbes (1588 - 1679). Hardin is mostly know for his analogy of 'The Tragedy of the Commons'. The 'tragedy' being that if everyone is responsible for a common resource, in reality no one is responsible, and so the property will soon be destroyed and none will profit. Without private property there will be a 'war of all against all', which had already been foreshadowed in the writings of Hobbes.

Transposing these notions of property to the realm of responsibility and joy, they are an analogy for the stake that every member of a given society has in the well-being of any other members. Instead of this mutual responsibility actually being no one's responsibility, quickly leading to destruction, it can be organised so that the possibility of joy is everyone's responsibility. A life well-lived is conducive to joy. Joy is at the basis of the most successful societies and the most successful species, because they are the ones that cooperate the most effectively with the greatest number of other species and societies. Cooperation presupposes mutual benefit, and thus, successful communities will strive for a mutually beneficial, joyful situation for all. If a single person is unhappy, then it is the task of the entire community to bring about their happiness. This will maybe lead to a situation that is less 'luxurious' for some, but it will by necessity also lead to a situation that ensures the greatest notion of justice, as well as joy, for all.

Let me illustrate this with a story.

The good merchant

In the city of Ur lived a merchant named Archus. He was a good man, father to three daughters with one woman, and father to one daughter with another woman, who also had two daughters with another man. All lived together in a house and there was much love between them. Trade was steady, and they lived without worry. Tradesmen from other parts visited Archus and many a meal was shared in his house.

A merchant trading in sheepskins came from Gomorra, a city where the people treated their animals very badly, and they themselves also had very little. The merchant showed Archus the skins he wished to sell. He said: As you know, my people do not have a good reputation. This pains me. Admittedly, many among them are unpleasant and blunt. The best you can say is they live their lives without causing much damage, but you and I know that avoiding damage is not the same as supporting your fellow man. I would say that they foresee in their livelihood for no other reason than that they desire life and not death. But they are the people I know best and I know them to be good people at heart. Poverty is to blame for their rudeness and were it not for poverty, they would most certainly be as well-tempered as you.

Archus asked: How can I help you?

The merchant said: What am I to you? I do not ask you to help me. But if you would sell the skins I brought, my people can have hope for a better life. I ask only that you sell these skins to your customers, and give me a price in accordance with your own earnings.

Archus looked at the skins and saw that they were of meagre quality. The wool was thin, the leather was tough, and some skins even showed scars from a whip. He knew the stories of the inhabitants of that city. He knew how they treated their animals, and he did not know what to do.

That night, he consulted the loved ones in his house, and he said: These people live in barren parts where the weakest carry the heaviest burden. If I accept their trade, I can sell it for a good price even though it is not of the best quality. The tradesman will be able to pay his people more than he can afford now, and this could be a great help to them.

The first woman, the wise Pharmakeia, replied: Our people are blessed. The earth gives us everything we need. We know this is a gift, and that we owe gratitude for it. That is why we thank the Goddess in our temples. We bring her sacrifices, and we look for her where we hope she is. In accordance with her commandments, we avoid cruelty towards people and animals.

But those who wish to trade with us now are not like us: They do no honour the Goddess. They treat their animals badly, everybody knows. They take what they can get and they do not strive to give anything in return. If we accept their trade and earn money on their behalf, does that not make us just like them?

The other woman, Sybille, who was also very wise, said: The people all come from the same wood. The Supreme Mind has given them their freedom and they have spread out all over the world. We, who live in deference to the Goddess, do not have the right to rule over others, not by means of violence nor by means of poverty, because poverty is nothing but another kind of violence. We can ask these people to respect our laws and treat their animals the way we know to be right, and if they are willing to do so, we can trade with them and give them what they desire.

Archus heard their words and he said: They offer these skins, they do not offer others. I shall sell these for them so they can make money. When I give them the money, I will request that they henceforth treat their animals like we know the Goddess desires us to. If, on the other hand, I refuse their trade, they shall not begin to live better lives, and the misfortune will subsist.

In the months that followed he sold the skins for the merchant. They were of lesser quality than his customers were used to and

Archus sold them at a low price. Because the merchant from Gomorra desired only a small part in equity, Archus nevertheless earned more than he did selling skins of better quality. Every time he gave the merchant his money, he asked him to urge his people to henceforth treat the animals better and not make them suffer. Yet every new shipment was equal to the last.

Archus' trade blossomed and was now even largely made up of the skins from Gomorra. He noticed that his customers less often bough the good skins, but this made no difference to him. The people of Ur, who were very good to their animals, did ask him why he preferred to sell bad skins, but he said: I would rather sell the beautiful wool of our own sheep, but I cannot sell what no one will buy. My customers prefer the skins from Gomorra, which are cheaper. But not to worry, this will pass. I urge them to henceforth treat their animals better, and their skins cannot remain so cheap when they do.

Despite Archus' reassuring words to the people of Ur, and despite his repeated requests to the merchant from Gomorra, very little changed. Through the years, Archus' trade blossomed and although his house had grown quiet, he was very prosperous. He left the trade in Ur to his servants while he himself traveled and sold the cheap skins in other cities as well.

When he returned from his travels, he would sit on his balcony and smoke. When he was in Ur, he took the time to visit the temple regularly, and he made sacrifices in accordance with the forms so that no one could say he was not a just man.

The shepherds in Ur could no longer live off the sales of skins. They sold their herds and moved away. The people that stayed behind became divided among themselves. They saw that the people in Gomorra prospered, even though they still treated their animals badly. Archus' servants delivered the money to the people in Gomorra, but they no longer asked them to observe the laws of the Goddess, because they knew these people regarded their own laws as higher, even though they were not just.

One day, Pharmakeia noticed that Archus was growing thinner and that his body displayed strange spots. Archus said that it would pass, but it did not pass, and he became thinner and thinner. He even weakened to the point that it finally seemed he would die, but he did not. He remained among the living even though he no longer left his bed.

This strongly divided the people in Ur. Almost all of the trade left to the city was in Archus' hands. If he were to die, they feared poverty for everyone, even though they knew he would not bring them new prosperity as long as he was alive.

Some said: We put the fate of Ur into the hands of one man, and now we are torn apart by our fear that this man will depart. But we were not unhappy before he came, were we?

Some said: What could happen to Archus could happen to any of us. Who says that there is not a warning hidden in his sorrow? Our city blossomed thanks to his ingenuity, and now it shall perish because of his misfortune.

Some even said that if the people of Gomorra could now afford greater luxury, they had, in fact, stolen that luxury from Ur. It was said that Archus had sold them out to the enemy and that they had the right to take back what had once been theirs.

The despairing citizens of Ur began to talk of war, even as they argued among themselves. Simple gestures were misunderstood, those who spoke of peace were mocked. Because no one understood what was truly dividing them, they became ever more angry, yet could not find a solution. Every group had its own leader who spoke of the injustices that had been done to them. Finally, a meeting was convened, where four leaders discussed what was to be done.

The first one who spoke was the sister of Archus. Her name was Promonthea. She said: My brother is an estimable man who has done much good. He brought trade to the people of Ur, he helped the people of Gomorra who were very poor, he traveled a lot and brought back knowledge and science. Now he is old and sick, which is eventually everyone's lot. The people of Ur should take him as an example, the way he was when he was strong, instead of jeering at him now that he is old.

The second one who spoke was Bonartus, an apothecary and a very pious man. He said: When he was well, Archus stopped visiting the temple. He was continually traveling or working, and when he finally returned he made his sacrifices after the time had passed. He had his reasons, but reasons are no excuse. He brought affluence to some, that much is true, but that affluence was not based on what we have always considered to be just. He has erred, and we have lost our way along with him. Perhaps it is not yet too late. We must return to the way we used to be, and learn from Archus what we must do differently.

The third one who spoke was a man named Epheuter, who had most of his friends among the seafarers. Epheuter looked all of them by turn in the eye and said: Some of us are fanatical about the old customs, others want to leave, some want to stay here to die, and you, Bonartus, you see the affluence as our virtue but its loss as the error of a single man, arguing that all will be well if we honour the Goddess properly. But why can't we face that we are on our own? The Goddess has abandoned us. The fate of our people no longer holds her interest. For a long time, we believed in the rituals that had been passed down to us, and we behaved as we believed we ought to. It has now become clear that living in accordance with the rituals had no other purpose than to bring harmony between our people. Now that there is no more harmony, the rituals have outlived their use. We must not rely any longer on the support of a Goddess we have never seen. Instead, do as the people of Gomorra do, and gear your behaviour towards what is profitable.

Hereupon the fourth, a young poetess named Peronea, burst out to him: If you can surmise from our misfortune that the Goddess has abandoned us, why do you think that you could surmise from our happiness that The Goddess Eleima was with us? Is she so easily recognised? Are you the priest who can tell us what Eleima herself refuses to say? Are you the prophet who can foretell the departure of the Goddess? Now that our existence is threatened, we must believe more than ever that the Goddess desires more from us than ignorant worship. Now that times are hard, more than ever before, we must trust that her laws are just and that we must act justly. If we were to know no adversity, our behaviour would be of little worth to ourselves as well. By giving us a choice, the Goddess Eleima is giving us the chance to show we are worthy of her guidance.

In the end they agreed that if Archus was the cause of the current dejection, they had to ask him why he had acted as he had, and that they had to ask him this before he was too far gone to answer sensibly. So, they hastened to him and asked him: Archus! You had the power to help the shepherds of Ur, yet you chose the people of Gomorra, a city that does not honour our laws. We have allowed you to do as you liked, to our own misfortune, yet we shall act towards you as we always have. When you die, we will burn the body you leave behind as the rituals dictate, but before you die, we ask of you to tell us why you have turned yourself away from the people of Ur.

And although the words came with difficulty, Archus said to them: My life was like a boat which I have sent to sea and the sea has transported me. Just like the sea does not refuse any rivers, so I have accepted the waves. I was always prepared to leave as soon as I arrived somewhere, and so I withstood the burden of a heavy existence. It is not up to me to resist what enters my path. I am but a humble merchant, I have little to choose. Who could ask of me to judge the people of Gomorra for what they were not? They asked for my help and I did not refuse it. The good people of Ur, the merchants from other cities, all have deemed the cheap merchandise from Gomorra suitable to their own purposes. I have offered the people a choice, and they have made their choice. Now my body is prematurely painful and ill. Perhaps I should see that as a punishment from the Goddess, although I have always honoured her. If you wish to know what you should do, then make a worthy sacrifice in a quiet place, and hope that she is willing to accept the sacrifice.

They decided to heed Archus' advice and have Epheuter and Peronea make a sacrifice in a secluded spot. The two went on their way and made the sacrifice in accordance with the rituals.

The omens were favourable. There was a mild breeze when they began their journey and a golden sun shone down on them while they said their prayers. On the last day, it rained down on the seeds of the sacrifice, and that too appeared very favourable. After three days had passed, they prepared to return to the city, but decided to spend one more night in the place where the sacrifice had been made.

That night, Peronea dreamt that she lived in a house in the forest. During the day, she heard the vague promises of the wind and the singing of the water. At night, she flew around like a bird longing to fly forever on. It was cold and her house offered her no protection. And as she flew there, she heard a voice. She opened her eyes and saw below her the shape of a wolf with manes as light as gold. The poetess flew to a low-hanging branch and placed herself in front of the mighty animal.

The wolf spoke: I am daylight. I am the air, I am fire. Wheresoever I go, all will be visible.

Peronea asked: Oh, mother of the earth! Shall you preserve your children?

And the wolf replied: Be diligent in doing good deeds, so that your legacy may precede you. But if fortune smiles upon you, do not be complacent, for as she has come into this world so shall she perish. Prosperity is like the rain and the sunshine. Do not be conceited because of your affluence and your wealth, because those, too, you will have to leave behind. It does not suit you to be arrogant because of the ties to your people, because your true nature is proven by your own actions.

The wolf came closer and Peronea felt the hot breath on her face. The wolf looked up with glowing eyes and said: Avoid pride because you are alive, because death visits all, and the strongest ones are the first to fall to the ground.

The poetess fled outside where her companion had made his bed on the moss. She told him of her vision and both hastened back to Ur. Upon their arrival they washed themselves in the river, put on clean clothes, and convened the others.

Once they were together, Peronea explained how the Goddess had appeared to her in a dream and they all said: We shall cease our fighting. Only Epheuter the seafarer said: The words of Peronea are not aimed at me. It is true that some have built their fortunes with the blood of others, and have seen it perish with their own, but it is also true that what applies to most does not have to apply to all. Those who refuse the wealth there is in the world act as haughtily and ungratefully as those who have gained their wealth in dishonest ways. If the city refuses to defend itself agains the blows of fortune, I and my family shall leave the city, and we shall try our luck elsewhere.

Peronea said: When the night falls and the prayers die out, and all you can see is the glance of a falling star in the distance, then think of what unites us. It is only hope that springs eternal. If you leave in despair, your flight will be short-lived.

The others asked him to change his position, so that he could support them in the trade with other cities, but Epheuter could not be swayed. Soon thereafter, he left the city, in his entourage the ships of family and of those who had chosen to join him. A strong wind rose immediately, sending him quickly towards the sea where many ships have perished.

The people that had stayed in Ur built new ships. They sailed out to the nearby cities and eventually to farther regions. After Archus had gone from them, they brought new cargo with their little boats, but they told the people of Gomorra that they would no longer trade in skins.

Before travelling to Utopia

The West is in trouble. Depending on your beliefs, you may think this is a good thing, but it is not. As the West is struggling, the rest of the world is suffering. No matter how good any individual may be at heart, collectively wo/mankind is striking at the very thing we depend upon. It's not merely problematic that this 'thing' happens to be our entire planet, and that it is wounded and maimed - although it obviously is - but it is also problematic that as an industrialised global community, we apparently are driven to furthering Evil instead of Love. It may not be our own fault, it may just be that the evil that is out there finds an easy prey in people who have lost their bearings.

'Society' may be what people think they have created, but no one person can take credit, and it's very likely that forces out there in the dark are using people to propagate their own longings. People can be anything, good or bad, but 'the evil spirits' can only be evil spirits and they can only strive for the spreading of Evil. So, society is not at war with itself, it is instead struggling to survive a force that has seemingly taken hold of the invisible world. The invisible world shelters many other spirits as well, which need our help as much as we need theirs. To remedy what has gone wrong, we need a new language, because we can only think about our actions if we have words to think with. This new language is The Faith of Eleima.

Within the old books, we have to conceive of a new book. Within the old societies, we have to build a new society. As reasonable, sentient beings, we have to expose and undermine the structures that are erected along the current road to nowhere. That very road itself needs to be broken into pieces, so that it can no longer cover up the river of love. This needs to be done in a manner which in itself does not further violence, but instead, demonstrates that those earlier structures were never in our best interests. We can't merely set up another society with a different government, we need to talk about how to re-organise society so that it becomes clear for all to see that violence does not serve us. And so, we need to change from the kind of people that we have been into a new kind of people.

The Faith is a tool to enable this change. It offers a language with which to communicate with each other, with ourselves, and with the Gods and Demons that rule our lives. By adopting the notion of a world of spirits within us and outside of us, yet independent from us as well, it becomes possible to imagine a completely new way of being. In essence, The Faith I offer up for your consideration wants to rewrite the Book of Longing. We may not be able to escape our human frailty, but we can find another way to perceive that frailty. We have the capacity to cause great suffering as well as to cause great happiness, so why not choose happiness and leave suffering behind? You are offered hope, why choose despair? We can use this Faith-tool to understand what we're dealing with, in order to be able to protect ourselves while we're in the business of creating The Good Life.

If you're thinking this sounds suspiciously like searching for a new Utopia, consider this. Why would striving for Utopia be less worthy than this so-called 'realism' that is touted by people who are either scared or are engaged in the political professions? After all, what is termed 'realism' doesn't offer a solution, nor does it show an alternative. What really is Real, is the problematic state of our planet, and the loss of any kind of framework to alter that reality. The term 'Utopia' on the other hand, does not have to be a hindrance towards achieving a more peaceful society on a blossoming planet. It's just a word, except that it's a word that points towards a brighter future.

The notion of Utopia has been discredited. It has been replaced by bleaker visions of economists, or of authors such as George Orwell and Aldous Huxley. These days especially, Huxley's 'Brave New World' is often touted as the model to avoid. Huxley painted a world in which people are happily drugged-up, and all dissent is smothered, thus leaving the fate of society in the hands of its rulers, who do as they see fit. In this brave new world, everybody lives 'the good life', but obviously, there is a catch. The scary thing about Huxley's vision is how his future society has been robbed of essential human characteristics as creativity and, paradoxically, hurt. Huxley understands that a certain amount of sorrow is needed to feel completely human, and this understanding has been adopted by many to spread the idea that a Utopia is not merely impossible, it is also undesirable. However, why would Huxley's vision imply that we have to go looking for sorrow? I've always had the impression that there's enough sorrow to go around, there seems little reason to assume we will run out one day.

The acceptance of life coming at you 'warts and all', has been a little over-emphasised of late. Some say 'hell doesn't sell', but it is my distinct impression that in this 21st Century it actually sells like hot cakes. With the popularity of Huxley's bleak vision, the idea of a society in which things have been organised in a way that makes for the happiness of all - that is: a Utopia - has fallen from favour. It seems nobody wants it to be an option anymore. I think this is because of the way in which all of us are constantly brainwashed by - dare I say it? Yes, I do - capitalist propaganda. I don't mean to go all radical socialism on yo ass, but the notion of the good life-as-consumer's-paradise is at least partly expressed through popular entertainment. That is because the entertainment industry is, in fact, an Industry. It strives for achieving the same goals as heavy industry, which is: To propagate the belief that people are singular beings, and that the best life is had through producing and consuming. The notion that life is not meant to be spent chasing after consumer goods, let alone meant for suffering through a job that gnaws at your soul, has been thoroughly discredited. And it's equal parts interesting and equal parts disheartening that nowadays most intellectual life in The West seems to be expressed through entertainment.

What popular entertainment adds to heavy industry is the promise of Love-as-Saviour. Through sounds and images, the notion of this saving grace is constantly reinforced. Romantic love is represented as the thing that will keep you from leading a life without meaning. When a life of consumption starts to seem hollow, then true love will come and save you, or so all of us are led to believe. In order for 'Love' to come and save you, all you have to do is live a life that does not set you apart from the others. After all, how can your One True Love find you if you're outside of the consumer's paradise? How can you be saved if you set yourself apart? And how can you find your place in society if society is not seen as the House of Industry whose walls will keep you safe? Without explicitly saying so, the mantra of entertainment and industry is 'find true love, work hard, live the good life'. In fact, this is the way the notion of a Utopia has been stolen from us, because rather than searching for a way of being that is joyful to all, this propaganda tells you that you have to be an individual worker in the bosom of society, so that you may be saved through love.

Even politics has become entertainment, and even politicians hold up the notion of 'Love' as your saviour. If it's not 'love of money' that is the jingle to whistle along to, then it is 'love for country' or 'love for your culture' that holds the promise of a new dawn. This has always been why the lure of fascism is so much more powerful than any of the other - isms. The Demon of Love takes on the guise of the beloved leader, the strong man who will come and save us all from the clutches of the unnamed hordes. It's still entertainment though, it just tries to entertain you through the idea of violence and aggression.

The promise of romantic love is made so as to keep everyone fixated on a very particular notion of the luxury life. But to my mind, true luxury does not merely combine goods and services into a pre-packaged vision of a group searching for this rather mediocre kind of happiness. True luxury comes with being in a state of tranquility, while completely aware of the abundance the world has to offer. My notion of a new Utopia comes with a sense of being able to touch upon the entire world, the world that The Liberator has shown. Luxury means that you feel you are connected to your surroundings, and that it makes sense that you are here. On the other hand, living a life in a world of connected electrical appliances is not so very luxurious, because there is an obvious difference between being connected to the internet of things and being connected to the Gods. So, as a society, we need to see beyond the images of entertainment and industry, and establish a new way to express the love-demon that is living in the invisible world.

I would like the mantra of society to say, 'See how you are connected with this living world that surrounds you. See how your actions have an effect that go beyond your individual self. Feel how your Self is trying to further the consciousness of the divine'. This new mantra will allow for the possibility to begin life anew. And surely, Love will still be able to find you, because Love is always out there, searching for you. Love is a Demon, she goes her demonic ways, just trying to be expressed. Love is not your saviour from a life that is only half-lived without her, and neither is Love a puppet in the puppet show of entertainment and capitalism.

There is a difference between Love as a tool, and being in love. Before we are collectively swept away by Evil, there is still time to built a new Temple, a temple of the mind, where the feeling of being in love can flourish. So I propose to collectively take a deep breath, and see what A New Utopia might look like. After all, if we are to find a new way of living, then we need a plan. 'Do yourself a favour, become your own saviour!' - as the late, great Daniel Johnston once sang.

Establishing a temple of joy

When you think of yourself, you may very well have an image that is a little vague, sort of like an overlay of people and clothes and houses and aspirations. You are a construct, the marriage of your personal history and your family history merging with the history of humankind and all the things you've heard and believed at one time or another. You are the face you see in the mirror, as well as the beating heart you feel on the inside. You are the laughter that suddenly bursts out, and you are the tears that well up in your eyes when you look at a picture of something that you think you've lost. You are a person at work, and you are that person asleep in your bed. You are your own feelings of nostalgia for an age yet to come. You are not at the mercy of anything, and you can transform into anyone you desire, even when it doesn't always feel that way.

Assuming this goes for all the others as well, in order to achieve any meaningful change, all these images need to add up into a conscious ideal. I imagine this ideal as a person that at their heart holds the notion of an intimate connection to the world of the Gods. When that intimate sense of connection comes together into a single image, it might be thought of as 'the temple'. But, as we all know, the Gods share their world with Demons and Spirits, so the intimacy that can be found may be inspired by feelings of Rage as much as by feelings of Joy - the temples that we need have to be constructed so that they can shelter us, while warding off the evil that may sneak in. After all, we don't want to build our temples and then find ourselves locked up in places where demons come to hide.

When it's everyone for themselves, it becomes very hard to avoid being roped in by demons presenting themselves as conflicting feelings inside of us. The spirits swirl around, and instead of allowing us to experience a continuous sense of joy, they lead us and our societies into the jaws of The Great Snake of Chaos and away from the Tree of Wisdom. So, we need to build temples where it's not everyone for themselves, where we feel we are all going through life together. There, the living undercurrent of the world may be reaching out to us, but we are strong in our connection to the Goddess that guides this world of people.

Taking a cue from ancient practices, I propose the building of 'a temple' in any place where such a temple can be. In these temples, people may get together and touch upon the reality of each other's experiences. After all, we have so many shared experiences and we have so many wishes in common, when becoming truly aware of this common longing for intimacy, it gets hard to see why the others ought to be denied what we long for in our own lives. The reality of being alive may be seen in these temples as providing the ability to see ourselves as we really are, not as these all-too human constructs, but as fragments of the Supreme Mind going through cycles of creation and destruction.

In these temples there will be music and dance, in a slow and hypnotising rhythm, in fact, there may be music that can hardly be recognised as music, because it is made up of the songs of birds and the humming of the earth. There will be a reading of texts, not as a stern reminder to be something you're not, but as a sharing of feelings through words that in themselves are endowed with feelings because they are shared.

Presuming it is joy that we're after, a conversation is needed to establish what each person's ideal 'temple' consists of. Then, because these notions may differ and there may be spirits out in the world that wish to influence our feelings in order to further other notions, there need to be rituals and celebrations through which the feelings themselves can be investigated. To illustrate this on a really rather mundane level, there is research indicating that judges tend to be less lenient before lunch. An empty stomach is not conducive to kindness, or so it seems. Therefore, in the temples there will be rituals performed that nourish the body and the soul. With a heart full of love and a belly with a cookie inside, it becomes much easier to express joy.

These temples can be anywhere, in fact, they can be inside of you. These are the altars the daughters of the Goddess Eleima have erected in the hearts of the people to honour The Unity. These are the temples where the daughters can be a guide to the people, and it is from here they lead all people back to their destination, where they shall be at one with The Unity, the eternal Mother-Father. In this temple, you needn't limit yourself to being your own saviour, you can be your own priest/ess, too!

The notion of A Temple, or of temples, brings with it the gathering of people. There is conflict enough in the world today, the temples can instead be places of peace. The following chapters will expand on ways to establish these temples and to find that kind of peace. After all, 'peace' is not a singular notion, there is not a cube-shaped bit of peace you can find lying on a shelf, just waiting for you to uncover it. The temple is the place where peace is found through a better insight into the ways we can actually lead our lives.

Non-violence

How does this all add up into a coherent, meaningful system?

Rousseau envisioned his Social Contract to work best in a small City-State. And sad to say, it's not very likely that a worldwide Utopia can be achieved in the foreseeable future. It seems clear that in order for the Social Contract of Joy to work, a first step will have to be a reduction of scale. Even though I'd like this movement to be a worldwide realisation that we have collectively been led astray, change takes time. First, we need to build temples of the mind, before we can build the new temples for people to get together and lead the good life.

We can conceive of the temples as micro-Utopias. The temples can be wherever small groups of people come together to try out for a new way of being. There can be a micro-Utopia when three or four people get together and sit in silence, holding hands, then maybe hold a little ritual such as dedicating the afternoon tea to the Gods. Just be together and be intimate, share the warmth of a body, then get back to the outside world again, knowing that there is a quieter way of being waiting for you.

This humble beginning could be much like the Amish practice of 'Rumspringa' turned inside out. During Rumspringa, the adolescents are free to venture out into the modern world to see for themselves which way of living they prefer. They can go to the city, play loud music, experiment with temptation. It is only when they subsequently wish to return to the Amish way of living that they may become a true member of that church and renounce the ways of modernity. Except that in the micro-Utopias, I think we can have many joyful ways open to everyone at all times. Why limit yourself to only one way of being when you can lead various lives at a time? It's just that in all these lives, you are a messenger to the Gods. In all these lives the notion should be present that you need to act in a manner in which you would like everybody to act.

In order to create a greater society out of these micro-Utopias, it's necessary to agree on a set of basic principles. And because any principle that doesn't allow for exceptions will at some time or other bump up against an unexpected situation, instead of thinking of these principles as rules or laws, they should be considered 'guidelines', similar to 'best practices'.

The first guideline needs to be concerned with 'Freedom'. On the one hand, The Good Life consists of a basic notion of freedom that includes freedom from hunger, fear, cold, pain, and want. It also consists of the more abstract notions of emotional, physical and intellectual freedom. Obviously, no one should try to achieve these kinds of freedom just for themselves. One wo/man's liberty cannot be another's prison. Freedom can only come about if it's on offer for everybody, because if it's not, then at the very least, there will always be fear. Creating one's own freedom without regard to the others is a form of violence, and acting violently will inevitably cause a backlash. After all, even the violent have to fear violence. It's just the same with emotional, intellectual and physical freedom. Freedom of movement of body or mind can only be restricted by violent means, which will inevitably lead to conflict. A lack of intellectual freedom will lead to emotional suffering, which in turn may lead to physical pain. Freedom of movement is indispensable, because there is always a desire to find yet another kind of freedom, and this desire should not be thwarted. So, 'freedom' must also include allowing for anyone to go wherever they want to go, be it in the mind, be it in the body. This kind of freedom is an indispensable component of the good life.

And so, this Faith adheres to the principle of non-violence, so that freedom can be furthered at no cost to others.

This principle extends to the natural world of which - excuse me if I'm over-stating my point - people are a part. It has to do so, because not granting sufficient rights to the natural world, and specifically to animals, will lead to the appropriation of resources. If for example, animals are not thought of as inherently free, they can be locked up as property. Once locked up, they have to be guarded, if only against danger and disease, and so they become a source of envy and worry. As for plants, they have to be regarded as friends at best and unwanted guests at worst. Again, they must be seen as inherently free, because otherwise certain desirable plants will be grown at the expense of other plants. On a very practical level, to deny plants an equal status can sustain the current practice of using poison and weed-killers to rule over the plant world, which has turned out to be A Bad Idea. Also, if plants and animals are property, they will take up land where no other people can have their animals, and where no other wild animals may live. So it's easy to see that violence against nature is inherently restricting the freedom of other people and other animals, thereby creating a chain of violent reactions. Violence can only lead to further violence, so the principal of non-violence by necessity extends to all.

Then the question arises, 'If nature has to be treated with the respect we accord to other people, what shall we live on?' The answer to that is practical more than it is principled. We need food and we need clothes. Everything in nature eats something else, we are no exception to this phenomenon. And, being naked apes, we need to shelter from the cold. When applied to the animal world, the principle of non-violence will have to mean that the animals should not be treated badly, may not be killed, and that nothing may be taken off them that they cannot do without. So, for example, we can eat eggs or use wool, because the chicken and the sheep will produce these with no cost to themselves. However, their lives are worthy, and so they should be allowed to lead good lives. If chickens are treated as if they were egg-producing machines, then the laying of eggs actually does come at great cost. It's not a good practice to torment the chicken, nor is it good practice to maim the sheep or take its coat in winter. Therefore, the followers of The Faith will avoid eating meat, and they will avoid all cruelty to animals.

Plants can be treated according to similar principles, although plants have a different sensitivity. They will grow where they can, and they will do so at the expense of most other beings. Plants are not to be mistaken for kindly creatures. Plus, and this is the good news, they actually enjoy being used, getting pruned, and being eaten. Presenting themselves as dinner is a strategy for propagation, with animals eating fruits and spreading seeds. Agriculture is not bad for plants - it shouldn't be bad for animals either - if it is practised while keeping in mind the interests of other beings. This includes the interests of the soil, seeing as it nourishes plants, and keeping in mind that we all go there eventually. If plants and soil are seen as a part of the living world that in essence ought to enjoy the same standard of living as people, then we will all profit by that. Also, it becomes rather obvious that an agricultural practice that relies on poisons and fertilisers is equivalent to feeding people nothing but junk-food and weight-loss pills. The latter practice is not to be mistaken with living the good life.

All in all, a guideline to treat people, plants and beasts in a manner that becomes them, could be this: 'Treat all that lives and all that is as equal. Treat what is smaller as that which is greater, and treat that which is greater as a loved one. Treat a loved one as a friend, and an enemy as a lost friend.'

Slow down

From the above, there is a direct link to Moses Maimonides, the medieval Jewish philosopher (1138 - 1204). Talking about the love for God, he wrote: "One's soul shall be knit up with the love of God such that it is continually enraptured by it." Earlier on, Epicurus-the-prophet said that through our actions we change the ways the Gods see us and we set an example to others how they can be seen. These two visions imply a love for all that is, because it all comes from the Gods, and in all that comes from the Gods an innate beauty can be seen. This beauty in turn inspires a sense of wonder and surprise, because true beauty never ceases to amaze, and when you take this beauty in, you cannot be anything but loving. When loving, you show others how they may be loved, and you show this through your actions.

Now, 'Love' is a word that tends to be bandied about, growing ever more meaningless if you let it. Just recently, you couldn't buy a packet of crisps without the label stating your greasy snack had been 'made with love', which in reality translated to 'you're never going to find romance, so you might as well eat greasy potatoes instead'. That is the kind of love we can do without. When talking about 'Love' - indeed, when merely thinking about the notion of Love - it is the meaningful act that matters. Eating a bag of crisps is not the same thing as showing kindness to your fellow beings. I am thinking of showing love when I think of the guidelines that we need.

Our actions are what the world sees from us. Buying constitutes an action, too. Sticking with those crisps, what matters is how the potatoes were grown, in what way they were processed, and who has flourished through that. How has the earth been rewarded for what it has given? Have the plants not been made to suffer through weed-killers and have the workers been properly paid? How is the packaging contributing to a better environment? This can all be taken into consideration while going through the buying process.

What it means to actively treat your fellow-beings with 'love' is that you need to be aware of the beauty that already is in the world, and that you can honour this beauty through awareness. Our society is geared towards consuming, and through inattentive buying an inattentive attitude is fostered. To show kindness means to be aware of what the greater implications of your actions are, not just in any single act, but in all aspects of everyday life. Kindness implies the expression of awareness through actions.

If Love is a demon that is independent from us, yet acting through us - and we feel it moving inside - then we are caught between Love and its opponents locked in a constant struggle to be expressed. In everyday life, this needs to translate to attentive living. This needn't be hard, you don't have to do anything other than what you're already doing, except, when involved in that whatever-it-is, you take time to pause and pay attention to what the action entails. Buying cheap crisps may implicate you in a chain of unfortunate actions that you really don't want to be a part of. This doesn't merely go for crisps, as I presume you already gathered.

So, I guess, part of The Faith is taking the time to consider your actions. It involves slowing down, in the literal meaning of the word. Whenever you find yourself hastily going through some routine, or preferring something cheap 'n' nasty over a better alternative that takes more time, then just close your eyes and breathe. You don't have to be a saint, you merely have to pay attention. Through attention, love for the beauty in this world of Gods is shown. When you have an option, always choose the option that furthers the beauty.

Maybe it doesn't seem like a very practical guideline: 'Slow down'. It is though, because it implies postponing all judgement and inherent actions. Because through our actions we also show the others how they can be seen, when we slow down, we show the others that they may slow down as well.

This slowness can influence life in a profound way, especially when you take it as literally as you can. When thinking of taking a plane for instance, you are really thinking about travelling at great speed. Maybe take a train instead. Maybe try to limit the time spent travelling. Maybe travel for shorter stretches. Maybe stay home and read a book. Slowly.

Do not hold a grudge

The principles share a common trait. They offer a means of finding inner peace on a day-to-day basis. Because, even though at first we will be moving in and out of our little Utopias, as time goes by, we want to establish a more lasting temple. To that end, we need to find peace within ourselves, so that it can radiate out. It's a little along the lines of the immortal phrase by John Lennon and Yoko Ono: "War is over, if you want it." There can be peace, but you are in charge of it, and vice versa, if you continue to fight, there will not be peace.

In most religious systems, in spite of what they may have led to throughout the ages, there are admonitions to not hold a grudge. Because, simply put, when clinging to the idea that you have been wronged in any way, you will not be free. The past keeps its grip on you, and out of the past demons will come forwards to haunt your nights. When you hold a grudge, your mind is occupied with thoughts of how things could have been, how they should have been, how something that you could have had somehow has slipped through your fingers. What's more, you feel this whatever-it-is has not simply eluded you, it has been taken from you by somebody else. The very nature of a grudge is that it apportions blame to outside forces. And then, when you blame someone, the only remedy available is to take some sort of revenge, which can take any form. Ultimately the wish for revenge can lead to war, history is rife with tales of conflicts that have lain dormant for 100 years, only to erupt when times got harder and a scapegoat was sought.

This also goes for our current woes. They are caused by someone else's actions. When early on, I gave the statistics for the decimation of nature by man's hands, I was not saying this was my own doing. I blamed the evil-doers, and rightly so. I didn't say I had any role in this sorry state of affairs, *au contraire, mon ami!* I was saying: This is what we're up against. The enemy is in our midst, we have been cheated by forces in society, by industry. We should hold a grudge, and we need to take revenge. I'm not in the business of pointing at scapegoats, but if I were, my business would be flourishing, there are plenty of companies out there that are to blame. And it's true, there are forces that are seemingly beyond any individual's control, and certainly beyond mine. I didn't go out and mow down rainforests, I didn't personally spray the fields with Monsanto's herbicides, so that soy beans might be grown cheaply and feed a cow, only for it to turn into someone else's sorry slab of cheap meat.

However, when I am being brutally honest, I cannot deny that I did profit off that. I wanted cheap everything, same as everyone else, and so something's had to give. I don't eat meat, but I wear leather shoes. Nature has been sacrificed, and its sacrifices have been made on my behalf, too. I have worked for companies that have their fingers in everyone's pie, and I have allowed for evil actions even though I knew they were evil. So yes, someone else may be to blame, but there is always something that you can do as an individual. And if you have any power at all, then you should use that power to do good. Holding a grudge is a means of not taking responsibility for one's own present, even if the past cannot be undone. If it's inner peace that we're after, we need to see that holding a grudge is simply another form of despair. Despair may seem attractive, but as a foundation for a new and better society it's really rather worthless. So, it may not be a highly original guideline that I offer, but I offer it nonetheless: Do not hold a grudge, for grudges obscure the sincere desires and cause the Heart to grow bitter.

In a broader sense this guideline is recommending that you shun the profits evil-doers offer. It also encourages you to find alternative ways of living within a system that comes at too great a cost. I'm only pointing this out, because I feel it needs to be said time and time again, although I know that many people have already started to seek alternative ways of being. I offer this guideline to help build a foundation for these alternatives, it becomes easier to see what you're looking for once you can formulate the direction to travel. This guideline intents to be a roadmap into hazy territory. 'Go forwards,' it says, 'see how you can extract yourself from the grip that demons of the past hold on you'. This guideline is, in fact, a roadmap to happiness.

Also, even though you might not agree, I think that to avoid holding grudges does not imply that we should just let things slide. When damage has been done, or indeed, when damaging actions are continuing, then we cannot idly stand by. It is the duty of good people to stop the demons that cause mayhem, and make sure the repairs that are needed are made. Coming back to the Social Contract of Joy, this means that as a collective and as individuals, we have an obligation to find solutions that will establish a new, more joyful situation. Holding a grudge doesn't bring joy, but putting a halt to a bad practice and making repairs does. In daily life, all of us should try to let go of anger and resentment, we can learn to see that the anger that lives inside of us is no different than the anger that lives on the outside. Anger begets anger, sorrow begets sorrow, grudges beget grudges - and Joy begets Joy.

Finally, in a broader sense, realising that 'to hold a grudge' is another way of propagating anger, also implies a sense of non-attachment. All of us, being made out of flesh and bones, will at some point leave the body behind. What we want while we're still here is not having to suffer. Although not all experiences need to be pleasurable, fear of suffering is really rather universal, I think. When something has been lost, the realisation of this loss can cause pain and thus suffering. On the other hand, you can't lose what you never possessed, and seeing that nobody can possess anything makes it easier to let go. Being attached to the things that once have been stands in the way of pleasant memories, in fact, attachment stands in the way of seeing what is truly good.

Some things have been lost, and we are all the poorer for it, while other things have merely disappeared. We need to distinguish between what is what, and not be attached to what is not.

Although we can enjoy pleasant experiences or suffer through unpleasant experiences, what we want is for our daily life to be worthwhile. It is a hopeless life on this earth if every day is the same day, with the expectation of the next day only being worse and an abundance of food only foreshadowing the expectation of hunger. That way, the young do not display their powers, and the seeds of new battle are present in all peaceful moments. So, the need to live a life that is worthwhile is more than a mere 'nice to have', this sense of life being worthwhile is a necessity.

The worth of a life cannot be expressed in material things, because material things may be impressive, but they are still mere add-ons. What makes life worthwhile is the notion of being connected to a circle of friends and lovers, and the knowledge that these friends will not hold a grudge when times are hard.

True luxury

From all this, it follows that there will probably be less luxury. This is not because luxury must always be avoided, but because a lot of the amenities that are considered 'luxurious' lead to greater poverty. Living in a way that leaves unusable trash in its wake is not a luxurious way of living. Taking from the earth without allowing that same earth to regenerate is not a sign of luxury. Being able to take life from any species in such a way that the species are threatened with extinction is not luxury. Instead, this way of living merely furthers the evil, it is a sign of weakness and carelessness. This implies that we will have to think about what luxury actually means.

True luxury lies in the ability to enjoy the abundance of what is around, now and in the future. This means a redefinition of what 'the luxury life' entails. So far, this book has tried to describe how to envision that luxury in order to find an equilibrium between a life in which little is needed and a life in which every possible joy can be found. Plus, of course, the Good Life consists of the possibility of actively furthering Joy for ourselves and to the benefit of others.

I think this can be summed up in one sentence that may serve as a guideline: 'Covet what you need, and resist that which is no better than what you already have.' This is another way of saying, try to lead a life that leaves you free to experience the riches of your physical presence. Life becomes more valuable when you feel that you are connected to the living world. Being surrounded by dead consumer goods takes you away from that connection.

In case anyone missed it, this Faith is as much spiritual as it is political. The kind of luxury that we are taught to seek comes at great costs to others, and it is gained by violent means. Politics have at their core an evil ideology when they allow for luxury at the cost of slave labour, depletion of resources, as well as destruction of the land. The leaders and politicians that seek to defend this ideology inevitably resort to violence against the very people whose interests they purport to serve. This policy of luxury brings with it bullets for all. These are the politics we're dealing with.

I believe achieving the kind of freedom I described would in practice lead to a rather luxurious situation. The reason for that is that everything in nature instinctively strives for harmony, and people are no exception to that rule. 'Harmony' however, does not mean that all unpleasant things can be avoided at all times, it merely means that whatever lives and dies does no damage beyond the damage that is an inherent part of staying alive.

Returning to Rousseau for a moment, in his writings he observed that the contract between citizens and state imposes new laws, including laws on safeguarding and regulating property. Rousseau also noted that there are restrictions on how that property can be legitimately claimed. For an example he gives three conditions for the possession of land. The first being that the land was uninhabited to begin with, the second that the owner claims only what is needed for subsistence, and the third that labour and cultivation give the possession legitimacy. When thinking of these principles in the framework of current-day protection of 'ownership', to my mind, it makes sense that ownership cannot extend beyond a certain reasonable possession of any resources.

We, the people, are not served by policies that defend the right to own anything at great cost and no joy to others. Neither does it do us any good to serve the ones that wish to legitimise this ownership, nor to enable enforcing this kind of possession. As things stand, we may not be able to meet the politicians and their leaders with the kind of violence that they are able to bear upon us, but this does not mean that we have to participate in their policies with all our might. From the simple rule of 'cherish the good, avoid evil' comes the notion that we have to cease to be a part of this all-consuming society insofar as we can. After all, the might of the powerful is built on the strength of people cooperating. The armies, the police, even the mindless consumers, they are all just poor people seduced into enacting or tolerating violence against other poor people. In essence, we have to see that we are fighting ourselves when participating in the protection of a luxury that is steeped in violence.

What is truly good is the company of friends and lovers and a shared meal on the grass in front of a temple. So, instead of buying a new plasma t.v., I suggest we all go out and break bread with our friends.

So you'd like to change the world?

You could be forgiven for thinking this Faith is an amalgam of personal idiosyncrasies, Indian philosophy and Greek myths, combined with a Marxist view of Capitalism and a splash of anarchy. It is that, and it is much more. The Faith of Eleima wants to change the world.

I realise that changing the world is not an easy thing to achieve. I'm often told you can't change society, let alone all societies the world over. With this, it is meant that you can't change the way millions of people think. I'm also told it's pointless to want to resist technology, because you can't stop progress either. This is what I hear about most things, that they cannot be changed or resisted, and either way, resistance is futile. To think otherwise is childish, or so some people will have you believe. However, I posit that we can change society, and that, in fact, we should.

These days, it's plain to see that society has spun way out of control, human industries are destroying the planet we all depend upon. So then, why would it be childish to try to change the world? The world is in desperate need of change. Besides, it's no so much 'the world' that needs to change, what merely needs to change is thinking of humans as some kind of extraordinary non-animals. While we're at it, I say, let's get at the root of the problem, and let's change the way of thinking about property and money as though they're more real than our interactions with the world of Gods and Demons. We can do that, because, as people, we can do anything.

And then, when you think about it, aren't we all constantly trying to change our worlds around us anyway? We try to change our world by buying new clothes, so that we will become more attractive. We read books and watch films, so that we may learn, and we expect this knowledge to change us into better human beings. Travelling the world, learning new skills, training our bodies. Even when we don't explicitly announce we are trying to change the world, all of us are constantly trying to modify ourselves, and through modifying ourselves, we are trying to change our surroundings. We want the world we live in to change, and the world is always changing, like it or not. So why would it be childish to notice that the transformation we see around us is the wrong kind of change, and, instead, we ought to strive for another kind of change?

It's clear that there's nothing childish about wanting to change this world. It's just that we're discouraged from seeing the bigger picture. We are led to believe that we are helpless in the bigger scheme of things. Even though as consumers and workers we are exploited on a daily basis, what we're actually told is that as people we don't matter. But it's simply not true. We matter, each of us matters. Everything we do matters.

The world is changing all around us. This is because society is changing. We ourselves are changing. Instead of feeling helpless, we should embrace change, just not the kind of change that's presented to us, the kind of change that's evil and furthers violence. We should strive for meaningful change, we should strive for changing in a way that is pleasing to both body and mind.

What we need to do is to take an honest look at the way we treat our fellow living beings, both human and non-human. We need to re-think what the good life consists of, because all of us want to live the good life. To this end, we need a new tool, and that tool comes with finding a new language for organising our private lives as well as our societies. When we learn to see that people are living in a greater world than the world of shiny, happy goods, then we can leave our belief in the benefits of the material world behind and learn to enjoy the benefits of the invisible world.

There's still time for change, we're still free to adapt our needs to what constitutes true welfare. As a society, we need to put our freedom to good use. The pursuit of freedom is evil if it's used to take liberty away from others, no society should have laws that take necessary freedoms away from the innocent, even if it's in the name of some greater good. No country may be free to wage war on another country. No political party should be free to deny entire sections of the population the freedom to pursue a meaningful life anywhere they please. Also, there are limitations to the acquisition of wealth. One person's wealth may not cause another person's poverty. No one should act in a way that harms others, and no one should try to profit of that. The profiteers are as much in the wrong as those who wish to profit of the profiteers.

All people strive for a good life for themselves and for their families. Of necessity, this pursuit is greedy, but this kind of greed is not wrong, as long as it doesn't destroy the land we all depend upon. Currently, the land we depend upon is in the process of being destroyed, same as the seas that have brought us life. Human greed is causing us to act in ways that are conflicting with our well-being, so we need to become less greedy.

The way out of our predicament is to treat all that lives and all that is as equal. It's easy to do that, once you see that all that is comes from a Godhead that has an interest in us realising this. Then it's easy to see that we live our lives in co-dependance with the other living beings, just as we need to seek harmony with the things we call inanimate but that in reality sustain life. When you keep that in mind, you change your daily surroundings and you change the world. You change the consciousness of a Godhead.

So, we're often told it is childish to want to change society, or to resist progress. What this means is that we're often told things that aren't true. We need to act, and we need to achieve meaningful change in our own lives. If each of us achieves meaningful change in their own lifetime, then society will change too, and that is exactly what we need. Change is now.

A beginning, an end

It all began with a car crash, a fractured heart, thoughts about the absence of Self, and obnoxious egotism. So it will end.

It's hardly a revolutionary idea to think there is a reality that consists of the living world such as we know it, and another reality that we do not know. This idea is present in all popular culture, where it is indirectly addressed as part of a fantasy world. The other world can be a realm from where kindly ghosts are guiding the living, it can be an alternative dimension, or even a place on earth that has somehow gone undetected. The slightly revolutionary realisation I had was that I could sense this underworld in my own life. To that end I almost had to die, but I feel that was a small price to pay.

The other world is no less real, it just doesn't conform to the current belief in a private economy of destructive capitalism and solitary emotions, and so, thinking about it has become an almost revolutionary act. Becoming aware of this, I found that there is a wealth of knowledge that has been either gathering dust or that has been relegated to the trash bin of the non-scientific. To think of this other world as a world of Gods and Demons may have gone out of fashion, but that's not to say that world has vanished. We ignore this invisible world at our own peril.

This 'reality behind the reality' has brought me in touch with the wealth that led me to the mythology that I have described in this book. I offer this mythology as a means of finding sanity. To believe in Gods and Demons gives a sense of belonging. Living a meaningless life in a hierarchical, violent, capitalist society, is the alternative, but that life does not need us. In fact, such a life will be our downfall. The problem we face is that, as a culture, we have lost the ability to talk about 'the other world' in a meaningful way. Without that lost language, we have become strangers to ourselves. It's easy to glorify romantic love stories, but ignoring the love that is going on in the world of the other living beings has led us into a netherworld where violent spirits rule.

Out there in the dark live desires and urges that will swallow us up whole if we do not have recourse to any greater reasoning. We need Gods and the Gods need us. Without living beings, the Gods are forever stuck in that world of mindless spirits flying about, and without Gods, people are at risk of falling prey to the Snake of Chaos. People and other animals enable the Gods to gain consciousness, and that divine Consciousness in turn enables us to sustain ourselves through harsh times. Therefore, we also have to deal with Demons.

Demons may be considered forces such as Love and Evil, but whatever the names, they are dangerous things. They are trying to use us for their own goals.

First there was nothing I say, and then there was the Godhead we call The Unity. From this Godhead came the God of the Material World and the Goddess of the Invisible World. People were born out of a great war between these Gods. Now, we are messengers to the Gods, and our daily battles with the Snake of Chaos are the messages we send. It is through this battle that we may see that what we need is to further kindness and friendship, so that the Gods may then show us friendship and kindness in return. When each of us returns to the Earth, we will arise out of that Earth again, born anew into a world in which the Gods will welcome us in their midst.

All that lives and all that dies is a part of who we are. We may not know what we're dealing with, but that is not to say that we are separate from the Life Force and the world of Gods and spirits. The Gods are still out there. While we're here in this human reality, alive in this day and age, we can learn to ward off the Demons and effectuate change. We can change from a life that is built on violence to living a life that is in accordance with the awareness that has been lost. Because we already have great knowledge of the mistakes that have been made in the past, we do not have to make those mistakes again.

As people, we are surely endowed with an individual sense of self, we have individual agency, enabling us to make choices that work out in everyday reality and that may have consequences for ages to come. While transitioning from living a life that is built on the defence of a violent luxury for some and great suffering for most, we can keep what is good, and we can leave behind what does not serve us. We can realise once more that we are part of this world of Gods and Demons, and then we will find the good life just waiting for us.

The body is the gate

There are many topics that follow from what I said before, and much can be criticised, I'm sure. Even though my Faith leads to a different kind of politics, it also leads to many questions. Most of these questions can be addressed, but if I even so much as tried, this book would be turned into a manifesto or a political program, and that way you'd be precluded from making up your own mind. I've had my say, now it's your turn, reader, to see how you wish to live in this world of Gods and Demons. I will leave you here with a story about the Goddess Eleima.

The Goddess Eleima is present at every birth. All people are reborn each moment with a different past each time.

The key to the future need not be sought, for everyone shall receive the key in every new moment. Every new moment there is a door that can be unlatched and once that door opens, there is the chance to pass the threshold and do something that has never been done before.

A person seldom knows what the choices are, they see the door but not the opening, they know the past and look behind for answers to future questions. Those who see the questions, but not the present, can easily lose themselves. Those who seek only answers and cannot leave a single question unanswered are like a ship with nothing but anchors.

The answers and the questions that are important originate outside of the body and find their likeness in the body. They exist within the body and seek the liberty to be without words. By looking within the body with the means that exist outside of the body, a world becomes visible that precedes the word.

After she had left the temple, the Goddess Eleima went to the sea. She walked past a house where three men were standing. Upon her passing they addressed her. One of them said: We are the last of this city, after us there are none. These fields were once full of grain and a family lived in every house, now the fields are barren and the people have gone. Who knows where they have gone, who knows what will become of us? You who have come from afar, please, do not pass us by unobserved.

A second man supplemented his words by saying: I was a father, I was a husband and a friend. With my boat I sailed the seas and I caught as much fish as I needed, and no more. I fulfilled my duties, and there was joy in fulfilling my duties. Now my children have left for a more fertile region, my wife has died and there is no one left that I am responsible for. What is left to me are these men I call friends, although we seldom speak. You, who have come from afar, please, do not pass us by unobserved.

Finally the third man came forward, and he said: On this earth the people are but servants of the Gods, we must show ourselves worthy of this world's glory day after day. Wars are being waged, but not by us. We are not the slaves of the warmongers. We do not go into battle like mute animals in service of the evil that dominates us, we are the masters of our own destinies. We are the creation of the great Mother-Father, we live our lives and we can be the best we can be or the worst we can imagine. But here, in this desert, we lack the power to be anything other than men desperately persisting. You, blessed one who have come from afar, please, do not pass us by unobserved.

Eleima looked upon them and she became aware of a hunger within her body. The men were old and young, they were still strong enough to strive for good lives yet experienced enough not to want too much for themselves. The skin that overlaid their muscles was as a blanket protecting the silent animal from the night; their muscles were supple and strong, capable of joining together the whole of their being while experiencing the power of the Unity as it allows itself to be known by the people on earth.

And she said to the men: People live in the darkness of their convictions. There are many types of knowledge and people attach themselves to them. Knowledge shapes the people, they become what they think they know. They want things they cannot grasp and understand, things they can buy and things they can repeat. Words are the means of describing the shiny things and creating the pleasure these things will bring, because as soon as there are no more words the world changes its shape. Without words there is the direct experience of a world no longer obscured by the awareness of the consciousness. In this direct experience man himself changes shape, so that he is no longer merely a body full of desires, but a wave that is absorbed into the ocean.

It is possible, without words, to know the understanding of the experience we must seek. It is possible, without words, to show that we must leave words behind. And it is true that it is enough to come together through nothing more than the will to be together in action. The action cannot be other than simple, it begins with seeing each other. The other not as they appear, but the whole that makes up the body, the head and the space surrounding that body. Realise that the Unity is visible in all spaces, and that the Unity is present in the merging of the spaces with all that lives and all that is. Know that the Goddess Eleima will not forsake her task.

She took off the cloth that she had wrapped around herself and put it down on the beach. In her nakedness she sat down upon it and with a gesture she invited the men to join her. She now said to them: You can seek and hope that there is something to be found. You can believe in truth, but it will be a lie to someone else. Whatever it is that you believe to be eternal and true, only through the labour of the body can the light of the Supreme Spirit shine. Share your bodies with me and let us be as one who is complete.

Without saying another word they merged their bodies and they were together for many hours. The men cast off their worries, because the body is the gate to the experience of the Unity. Their selfishness tormented them no longer, they gave what they could give, they received what they could receive. Eleima, too, gave what she could give and accepted what was offered to her.

In the night Eleima left the men behind, after she had spoken to them in their dreams. She said unto them: This world is not the real one, she is in constant motion, a dividing line between what has been and the world that lies beyond it.

In this world no one can find peace by not acting on what they know, but they must not forget what has not been learned. Those who seek to truly live, see that life is contained within the body and that the body is not a treasure to be locked up, neither the body of a man nor the body of a woman. The body of a person is their life on earth, there is no person without this body, therefore the body must be cherished and it must be used. Within the body lies the Eternal Heart, the body is always and only for the Heart that is within the body. The body in harmony with a pure Heart can do anything, knows everything, always goes where it must go. Therefore, teach your Heart and have no fear. Perform your actions with the wellbeing of others always on your mind, share what can be shared. That which is scarce will prove to be abundant. What once was plentiful will be plentiful once more.

One last thing

My car did not live to tell the tale. Shortly after crashing, it gave out. On the bright side, the Demon of Love is still with me. All of which leads me to a final thought: Do not be worrisome, because a person is not determined by their worries. Worries merely take the colour out of life and make all days tasteless.

* * *

Visit www.eleima.org

Thank you

The ideas in this book have many authors,
known and unknown, human and divine.

Thank you for being beautiful: Lotte,
Anna, Peter, Madlen.

Further reading

I was much inspired by David Graeben, 'Fragments of an anarchist anthropology' (Prickly Paradigm Press, Chicago). The story of the Piroan people and their dangerous gods was lifted from this book.

A quick way of reading up on Rousseau is through simply finding a good book about all the philosophers of the Enlightenment. I recommend Isaiah Berlin's 'The Age of Enlightenment: The 18th Century Philosophers' (Plume publishers)

The Greek Myths come in many variations. A good overview can be found in this book by C. Kerényi, 'The Gods of the Greeks' (Thames&Hudson, London)

Soundtrack

Leonard Cohen - Here it is

Bob Dylan - Idiot Wind

Ed Kuepper - By the way

The Go-Betweens - Love goes on

Yames Yorkston & Adrian Crowley - Don't Let The Sun Go Down On Your Grievances

The Buzzcocks - Nostalgia (for an age yet to come)

The Plastic Ono Band - War is over (if you want it)

Lloyd Cole - So you'd like to change the world

Heaven 17 - Brothers! Sisters! We don't need this fascist groove thang

Jonathan Richman - Affection

www.ingramcontent.com/pod-product-compliance
Lightning Source LLC
Chambersburg PA
CBHW071703090426
42738CB00009B/1638